BETTY CROCKER'S
LOW-CALORIE
COOKBOOK

Golden Press/New York
Western Publishing Company, Inc.
Racine, Wisconsin

Photography Director: Stephen Manville
Illustrator: Roland Rodegast

Second Printing in This Format, 1978
Copyright © 1978, 1973 by General Mills, Inc., Minneapolis, Minnesota.

Printed in the U.S.A. by Western Publishing Company, Inc.
Published by Golden Press, New York, New York.
Library of Congress Catalog Card Number: 73-83923

Golden® and Golden Press® are trademarks of Western Publishing Company, Inc.

CONTENTS

Dear Calorie-Counter,

The secret of your success? Simple. Cutting calories in such a way that no one notices they're missing. The point is, calorie-counting shouldn't mean doing without. It should mean doing things differently. We're talking about a constant, not a sometime, thing. We're talking about planning differently, cooking differently, eating differently—and it's all easier than you'd believe. That's what this book is all about. How you can slim down, shape up, or simply hold the line and still enjoy foods you and your family love.

Would you believe salads shining with dressing, potatoes without guilt, desserts that look calorie-laden but aren't? You'll find dozens and dozens of recipes in these pages, each one pared—by a substitute ingredient, an alternate cooking method, a lesser amount of some ingredients, or any combination of these—to a new low in calories.

To start you off, we've put together menus guaranteed to be family-pleasers and calorie-counted for your convenience. In case yours is a house divided (as are most), there are hints on how to make one meal do for both calorie-counters and the rest of the family. And as an added bonus, we've suggested plans for putting our recipes together to make festive fare for your guests without breaking training for you.

There's a complete rundown of daily nutritional needs plus comparative calorie lists to show you where you're safe in "eating hearty" and where you'd better watch your step. And throughout the book we've sprinkled hints to help you out at calorie-counting stress points.

In short, we've tried to point you in the new direction. And once you've caught the spirit, we predict you'll want to branch out on your own. By using these guides to create your own dishes and your own special menus, we *know* you'll reap compliments for your food, and your family will be healthier and happier.

Sincerely,

Betty Crocker

YOU CAN DO IT!

Something triggered your decision. Maybe an uncomplimentary remark about your weight. Or the sight of your not-trim self in a 3-way mirror. It hardly matters. What counts now is your determination to lose weight—starting right now. You've taken your first step in the right direction. Now let's begin:

☐ Set a target date and start! Don't let anything deter you. The sooner you start, the sooner you'll be at your desired weight.

☐ Check with your doctor before you begin. Never cut calories to less than 1200 a day without a medical go-ahead!

☐ Set reasonable goals, never more than a pound or two a week. (Be realistic so you won't get discouraged!) And remember—not everybody can or should wear the smallest size the stores carry.

☐ Find a friend who'll count calories with you. Sympathetic support is the dieter's greatest ally—besides, it will keep you from boring the rest of the world.

☐ Pose for three candid snapshots—front, side and back views. No matter how awful, keep them. Repeat the snapshot routine in 30 days as visual proof of the progress you've made.

☐ Memorize "What Is Meant by a Serving?" (page 7). The sizes of portions can make or break your diet. Get an inexpensive scale and weigh everything before you put it on your plate. (Not as tedious as it sounds—after a little while, you'll be able to recognize too-big portions on sight.)

☐ Chart the essential food groups (see pages 6 and 7) and the number of daily servings you need of each. Keep track of everything you eat in a handy pocket-size notebook.

☐ Stock up on coffee, tea, low-calorie soda pop, instant bouillon, vegetable juices, nonfat dry and evaporated skim milk. Provision the refrigerator with vegetable snacks. These emergency rations can very well prove to be your survival kit.

☐ Get some graph paper to record your weekly weight loss—it's pure pleasure to watch it plummet. For more fun, mark in special rewards at certain loss levels—"2 pounds: Magazine subscription." "5 pounds: Theater tickets." "10 pounds: Brand-new clothes!" (You'll need some by then.)

☐ Think thin—you'll be surprised what a difference it can make. Good luck!

HOW MUCH CAN A CALORIE-COUNTER EAT EACH DAY?

Everyday variety is important. These are total servings, but they can be spread over breakfast, lunch and dinner according to your personal likes. Be sure that you include the servings required for each type of food every day—no more, no less.

Food	1200 Calories Daily	1500 Calories Daily
Meat, Fish, Poultry, Eggs	3 small servings (total 7 ounces cooked weight)	3 small servings (total 7 ounces cooked weight)
Fruits	2 servings	2 servings
Vegetables	2 servings	2 servings
Cereals, Breads	4 servings	5 servings
Milk	2 cups fortified skim milk	2 cups whole milk*
Extras	1 serving	3 servings

If you're consuming 1500 calories a day and you drink skim milk, you can have a total of 7 servings in the Extras category.

HOW TO MAKE YOUR OWN DAILY CHECK-OFF CHART

Food	Breakfast	Lunch	Snack	Dinner	Required Servings
(List food groups from chart above in this column.)		(Leave these columns blank and check off servings under the right heading as you eat them. Total the columns each day to see which food groups you've missed.)			(In this column, list servings required to fit your calorie needs.)

WHAT IS MEANT BY A SERVING?

Here are some examples. Each of these items is one serving:

Meat, Fish, Poultry, Eggs*
- ☐ ¼ pound (before cooking) boneless raw meat
- ☐ 2 slices (4 x 2¼ inches each) or 3 ounces cooked meat or fish
- ☐ 1 cooked hamburger, 3x½ inch
- ☐ 1 cooked small chicken leg or thigh

*1 egg can be substituted for 1 ounce meat

Fruits, Vegetables
- ☐ 1 medium fruit (apple)
- ☐ 2 small fruits (apricots, prunes)
- ☐ ¼ cantaloupe
- ☐ 10 to 12 cherries or grapes
- ☐ 1 cup fresh berries
- ☐ ½ cup fresh, canned or frozen unsweetened fruit or juice
- ☐ ½ cup cooked vegetable
- ☐ 1 cup raw leafy vegetable

Cereals, Breads
- ☐ 1 slice bread or small dinner roll
- ☐ 1 ounce ready-to-eat unsweetened iron-fortified cereal (about 1 cup)
- ☐ ½ cup cooked cereal
- ☐ ½ cup cooked rice, cornmeal, macaroni, noodles or spaghetti

Milk
- ☐ 1 cup milk (8 ounces)

Extras
- ☐ 1 teaspoon butter, margarine or oil
- ☐ 1 teaspoon salad dressing
- ☐ 6 nuts (almonds, cashews, walnuts)
- ☐ 35 calories of another food

The servings noted in this book are all reasonable portions for the calorie-counter. If you're cooking for a hungry family or guests, reckon on fewer servings per recipe, or double the recipe!

WHAT SHOULD A CALORIE-COUNTER CHOOSE?

	Choose	Avoid or Eat Sparingly
Meat, Poultry, Fish, Eggs	Very lean, well-trimmed meats Poultry and fish without skin Broiled or baked foods	Fatty meats, cold cuts, frankfurters Panfried or deep-fat fried foods
Fruits	Fresh, unsweetened canned fruits or juices; fruits rich in vitamin C (oranges, grapefruit, strawberries, cantaloupes)	Fruits in heavy syrup; fruit fritters
Vegetables	All vegetables; fresh, plain, frozen or canned (eat less often: corn, kidney and lima beans, peas, potatoes, winter squash)	Vegetables in sauces or deep-fat fried
Cereals, Breads	Whole grain, enriched, re-stored or fortified cereals and breads	Muffins, pancakes, waffles, biscuits, doughnuts
Milk	Fortified skim, buttermilk, nonfat dry milk Dry or 2% creamed cottage cheese, farmer or pot cheese, Neufchâtel and other low-calorie cheeses	Whole milk Cream
Extras—only after you have your required servings (see page 6) in the groups above	Low-calorie gelatins Desserts made with skim milk Egg whites Low-calorie whips Cocoa powder Angel food cake Desserts in this book Popcorn without added fat Low-calorie jams, jellies, syrups Mock Mayonnaise (page 40) Butter, margarine, mayonnaise	Whipped cream Chocolate Fudge, caramels Most cakes Ordinary pies, cookies Fried or deep-fat fried snacks Jams, jellies, syrups Rich gravies, sauces

MEATS AND MAIN DISHES — THE HEARTY HEART OF YOUR MEAL

Or
How to Make the Main Event Memorable

When anyone asks, "What's for dinner?" they really mean what meat or chicken or seafood is going to do the star turn at the meal. For this chapter, we've chosen bountiful dishes to delight the taste and still give you and your family vital protein, all the while whittling away at excess calories.

PARTY ROUND STEAK

2-pound beef round or family
   steak, 1 inch thick
1 can (4 ounces) mushroom stems
   and pieces, drained
¾ cup dry red or white wine
1 teaspoon salt
1 teaspoon lemon pepper

Diagonally slash outer edge of fat on meat at 1-inch intervals to prevent curling when meat cooks (do not cut into lean). Place meat and mushrooms in shallow baking dish. Mix wine, salt and lemon pepper; pour over meat. Cover and re-frigerate 8 hours, turning meat 2 or 3 times.

Set oven control at broil and/or 550°. Place meat on rack in broiler pan. Broil with top 3 inches from heat 7 to 8 minutes on each side for medium-rare. Heat mushrooms and wine in small saucepan.

Trim fat from meat; cut meat diagonally into slices and serve topped with mush-rooms and wine.

8 servings/185 calories each.

Take advantage of tenderizers. There are many commercial ones, seasoned or unseasoned, that let you broil lean, tougher meats beautifully.

BEEF-TOMATO CURRY

½-pound beef flank or round
   steak, cut into ½- to ¾-inch
   pieces
1½ teaspoons instant beef bouillon
½ cup water
2 large tomatoes, peeled and cut
   into wedges (about 1½ cups)
1 green pepper, cut into 1-inch
   squares
2 medium onions, cut into
   wedges
1 teaspoon curry powder
1 tablespoon sugar
1 tablespoon cornstarch
1 tablespoon water
1 can (16 ounces) Chinese
   vegetables
¾ teaspoon salt

Use large skillet with non-stick finish or coat regular skillet with vegetable spray-on for cookware. Cook and stir meat and bouillon in skillet until meat is brown. Remove meat; set aside.

In same skillet, heat ½ cup water, the tomatoes, green pepper, onions, curry powder and sugar to boiling, stirring occasionally. Cover and cook over medium-high heat 3 minutes. Stir in meat; heat, stirring constantly, until hot, about 1 minute.

Mix cornstarch and 1 tablespoon water; stir into meat mixture. Cook, stirring constantly, until mixture thickens and boils. Boil and stir 1 minute. Keep warm over low heat. In saucepan, heat Chinese vegetables (with liquid) to boiling; drain and sprinkle salt on vegetables. Serve meat sauce on Chinese vegetables.

4 servings/155 calories each. (Each serv-ing: about 1 cup meat mixture, ½ cup Chinese vegetables.)

GINGER BEEF

This savory steak is very simple to make. Saving idea: Buy a chunk of gingerroot and freeze it; then slice off pieces as you need them. Fresh ginger flavor—anytime.

 2 pounds beef round steak, ¾ to 1
   inch thick
 2 cloves garlic
 ½ teaspoon salt
Dash pepper
 1 can (10½ ounces) condensed
   beef broth (bouillon)
 2 tablespoons cornstarch
 ¼ cup water
 1 tablespoon soy sauce
 ¼ teaspoon crushed gingerroot
   (1 thin slice) or ⅛ teaspoon
   ground ginger
 1 package (7 ounces) frozen
   Chinese pea pods
Hot Cooked Rice (right)

Trim fat from meat; cut meat into thin strips, 2 x ¼ inch. Peel garlic and make several cuts on one end of each clove to release flavor.

Use large skillet with non-stick finish or coat regular skillet with vegetable spray-on for cookware. Cook and stir garlic in skillet until brown. Remove garlic and discard. Brown meat in skillet over medium-high heat, stirring occasionally. Sprinkle with salt and pepper. Stir in broth; heat to boiling. Reduce heat and simmer uncovered until meat is tender, 10 to 15 minutes. (Add small amount of water if necessary.)

Mix cornstarch, water and soy sauce; stir into meat mixture in skillet. Cook, stirring constantly, until mixture thickens and boils. Boil and stir 1 minute. (Gravy will be thin.)

Stir in gingerroot and pea pods. Cook, stirring occasionally, until pea pods are crisp-tender, about 5 minutes. Serve on rice.

8 servings/220 calories each. (Each serving: ½ cup meat mixture, ½ cup rice.)

Hot Cooked Rice
2⅔ cups boiling water
1⅓ cups uncooked regular rice
 1 teaspoon salt

Heat oven to 350°. Mix all ingredients thoroughly in ungreased 1- or 1½-quart casserole or in baking dish, 12 x 7½ x 2 inches. Cover tightly with aluminum foil and bake until liquid is absorbed and rice is tender, 25 to 30 minutes.

4 cups cooked rice/115 calories per half cup.

MARINATED CUBE STEAKS

 4 beef cube steaks
   (about 4 ounces each)
 ¼ cup low-calorie blue cheese or
   Italian dressing
 1 medium tomato, cut into eighths
Salt

Use large skillet with non-stick finish or coat regular skillet with vegetable spray-on for cookware. Place meat in skillet; pour dressing over meat. Cover and let stand 20 minutes, turning once.

Brown meat in skillet over medium-high heat about 4 minutes on each side. About 2 minutes before meat is done, add tomato. Season with salt. Serve meat topped with tomato and pan juices.

4 servings/250 calories each.

MEAT LOAF RING WITH TWIN BEAN FILLING

½ cup soft bread crumbs
⅔ cup skim milk
1 egg
1¼ teaspoons salt
1 pound lean ground beef
½ cup finely chopped onion
1 cup finely shredded carrot
¼ cup finely chopped green
　　pepper
⅓ cup chili sauce
1 can (8 ounces) cut green beans
1 can (8 ounces) cut wax beans
Lemon pepper
½ cup chili sauce

Heat oven to 350°. Use 5-cup ring mold or loaf pan, 8½ x 4½ x 2¾ inches, with non-stick finish, or coat regular ring mold or loaf pan with vegetable spray-on for cookware. Mix bread crumbs, skim milk, egg, salt, meat, onion, carrot, green pepper and ⅓ cup chili sauce thoroughly. Spread mixture in ring mold. Bake until done, about 1 hour. Drain off fat.

Heat green and wax beans (with liquid) to boiling; drain. Season with lemon pepper. Loosen meat from side of mold; unmold onto serving platter. Spread ½ cup chili sauce on top; spoon beans into center of ring or around loaf.

6 servings/240 calories each. (Each serving: 1/6 meat loaf, ⅓ cup beans.)

BEAN SPROUT BURGERS

Versatile ground beef and Oriental ingredients—an interesting combination of textures and flavors. Pictured on page 38.

2 pounds lean ground beef
½ cup bean sprouts, coarsely
　　chopped
½ cup water chestnuts, finely
　　chopped
1¾ teaspoons salt
2 teaspoons soy sauce

Mix all ingredients thoroughly. Shape mixture into 8 patties, each about 3½ inches in diameter and ¾ inch thick.

Set oven control at broil and/or 550°. Place patties on rack in broiler pan. Broil with tops 3 inches from heat about 5 minutes on each side for medium burgers.

8 servings/190 calories each.

CHILI WITH YELLOW BEANS

1 pound lean ground beef
¼ cup chopped onion
1 can (16 ounces) tomatoes
1 can (16 ounces) cut wax beans,
　　drained
1 can (10¾ ounces) condensed
　　tomato soup
¼ teaspoon pepper
1 teaspoon salt
1 teaspoon chili powder

Cook and stir meat and onion in large skillet until meat is brown. Drain off fat. Stir in remaining ingredients; heat to boiling. Reduce heat; cover and simmer meat mixture 25 to 30 minutes.

6 servings/190 calories each. (Each serving: 1 cup.)

NO-NOODLE LASAGNE

Keep all the lush lasagne flavors, but cut the calorie cost drastically by substituting zucchini slices for noodles. The family will want seconds of this. Pictured on page 37.

- 1 pound lean ground beef
- 1 can (15 ounces) tomato sauce
- 1½ teaspoons garlic salt
- 1 teaspoon basil leaves
- 1 teaspoon oregano leaves
- 1 carton (12 ounces) dry cottage cheese (1½ cups)
- ¼ cup grated Romano cheese
- 1 egg
- 1½ pounds zucchini, cut lengthwise into ¼-inch slices
- 2 tablespoons flour
- 1 package (4 ounces) shredded mozzarella cheese
- ¼ cup grated Romano cheese

Heat oven to 350°. Cook and stir meat in large skillet until brown. Drain off fat. Stir in tomato sauce, garlic salt, basil leaves and oregano leaves; heat to boiling. Reduce heat and simmer uncovered until mixture is consistency of spaghetti sauce, about 10 minutes.

Use baking pan, 9 x 9 x 2 inches, with non-stick finish or coat regular baking pan with vegetable spray-on for cookware. Mix cottage cheese, ¼ cup Romano cheese and the egg. Layer half each of zucchini, flour, cottage cheese mixture, meat sauce and mozzarella cheese; repeat. Sprinkle ¼ cup Romano cheese on top. Bake uncovered 45 minutes. Let stand 20 minutes before serving. Cut into squares.

9 servings/240 calories each.

DO-IT-YOURSELF TACO FEAST

- 1½ pounds lean ground beef
- 1 envelope (1¼ ounces) taco seasoning mix
- ½ teaspoon salt
- 1 cup water
- 12 ready-to-serve taco shells
- ¾ cup shredded lettuce
- ¾ cup chopped tomato
- ¾ cup chopped green pepper
- ¾ cup chopped onion
- ¾ cup chopped cucumber
- ¾ cup shredded Cheddar cheese

Taco sauce

Cook and stir meat in large skillet until brown. Drain off fat. Stir in taco seasoning mix, salt and water; heat to boiling. Reduce heat and simmer uncovered 15 to 20 minutes, stirring occasionally. While meat simmers, heat taco shells on ungreased baking sheet in 350° oven 3 to 5 minutes.

Spoon ¼ cup meat mixture into each taco shell. Add 1 tablespoon each lettuce, tomato, green pepper, onion, cucumber and cheese. Top with taco sauce.

12 tacos/190 calories each.

Beef groundwork. Recipes in this book are based on lean ground beef. It costs a bit more, but shrinkage is less, and it contains up to 20% less fat than regular ground beef. You needn't add fat for cooking, either, if you use a pan with a non-stick finish or coat your skillet with vegetable spray-on for cookware. More fat-losing facts: Always drain any fat from meat while it's cooking; grilling or rack-broiling lets fat drip off and away.

STUFFED GREEN PEPPERS

    6 large green peppers
    5 cups boiling water
1½ pounds lean ground beef
    2 tablespoons chopped onion
    1 teaspoon salt
    ⅛ teaspoon garlic powder
    1 cup cooked rice
    1 cup tomato juice
    6 thick tomato slices
Salt

Cut thin slice from stem end of each pepper; remove all seeds and membranes. Cook peppers in boiling water 5 minutes; drain.

Heat oven to 350°. Cook and stir meat and onion in large skillet until meat is brown and onion is tender. Drain off fat. Stir in 1 teaspoon salt, the garlic powder, rice and tomato juice; heat to boiling.

Lightly stuff each pepper with ½ cup meat mixture. Stand peppers upright in ungreased baking dish, 12 x 7½ x 2 inches. Cover with aluminum foil and bake 45 minutes. Top each pepper with a tomato slice and sprinkle with salt. Bake uncovered 15 minutes.

6 servings/255 calories each.

TOMATOED LIVER STRIPS

    1 pound sliced beef liver, cut into
        1-inch strips
    1 teaspoon instant beef bouillon
    ½ small onion, sliced
    ½ cup tomato sauce or chili sauce

Use large skillet with non-stick finish or coat regular skillet with vegetable spray-on for cookware. Cook and stir meat and instant bouillon in skillet over high heat until meat is brown. Stir in onion and tomato sauce. Reduce heat; cover and cook over medium heat until meat is done, about 5 minutes.

4 servings/170 calories each with tomato sauce; 195 calories each with chili sauce.

CHINESE PORK TENDERLOIN SLICES

Nifty now-or-later meat. Marvelous marinated pork to serve sliced in sandwiches or cubed in Super Supper Salad (page 16).

    1-pound pork tenderloin
    ¼ cup soy sauce
    1 tablespoon catsup
1½ teaspoons vinegar
    ⅛ teaspoon pepper
    1 clove garlic, crushed

Cut meat lengthwise in half. Mix remaining ingredients in medium bowl. Add meat and turn to coat all sides. Cover and refrigerate, turning meat occasionally, at least 8 hours.

Place meat on rack in roasting pan and bake in 350° oven 50 minutes. Cut into ¼-inch slices. Serve immediately or wrap in aluminum foil and refrigerate (up to 4 days) or freeze and use as desired.

About 64 slices/15 calories each.

PORK ROLL

Keep a cool but wonderfully aromatic kitchen by cooking this lean pork roast on top of the range. Press meat and slice for sandwiches; use skimmed broth for German-style Vegetable Soup (page 64) the next day.

1 teaspoon salt
½ teaspoon ground allspice
½ teaspoon pepper
½ teaspoon sage
3-pound rolled pork loin roast
6 whole cloves
4 cups water
2 cups ½-inch slices celery
1 tablespoon instant minced onion
2 bay leaves
6 peppercorns
6 whole allspice

Mix salt, ½ teaspoon allspice, the pepper and sage; rub on meat. Insert cloves in meat. Place meat and remaining ingredients in Dutch oven; heat to boiling. Reduce heat; cover and simmer 1½ hours, turning meat once or twice.

Remove from heat; leave meat in broth in Dutch oven. Cover meat with a plate; place a heavy weight on the plate (to press meat while it cools).

When cool, remove meat from broth and remove string. Cut meat into ¼-inch slices. Serve immediately or wrap in aluminum foil and refrigerate (up to 4 days) or freeze and use as desired. Strain broth into bowl; cover and refrigerate (up to 2 days) and use as desired.

About 22 slices/110 calories each.

PINEAPPLE PORK CHOPS

4 lean loin pork chops, ½ inch thick
1 can (8 ounces) sliced pineapple in unsweetened pineapple juice, drained (reserve 3 tablespoons juice)
⅓ cup soy sauce
¼ teaspoon monosodium glutamate
¼ teaspoon garlic powder
Paprika
Parsley

Trim fat from chops. Place chops in ungreased baking dish, 8 x 8 x 2 inches. Mix reserved pineapple juice, the soy sauce, monosodium glutamate and garlic powder; pour over chops. Cover and refrigerate, turning chops once or twice, about 8 hours.

Heat oven to 350°. Top each chop with a pineapple slice; sprinkle with paprika. Cover tightly with aluminum foil and bake until done, about 45 minutes. Uncover and bake 5 minutes longer. Remove chops with pineapple slices to serving platter; garnish with parsley.

4 servings/300 calories each.

Be a lean-meat cook. Trim off fat before you bake, broil, roast or stew. Chill homemade stews and soups; skim the fat from the top and discard, then reheat the mixture. Skin chicken and fish before cooking or before eating.

PORK CHOW MEIN

Splits up splendidly—calorie-counters eat it served over bean sprouts, hungry family members heap it on crisp fried chow mein noodles. Pictured on page 36.

1-pound pork tenderloin
1 cup sliced celery
1 medium onion, chopped (about
    ½ cup)
3 tablespoons soy sauce
1 teaspoon monosodium
    glutamate
2 teaspoons instant beef bouillon
    or 2 beef bouillon cubes
2 cups water
2 tablespoons cornstarch
1 can (3 ounces) sliced mushrooms,
    drained (reserve ¼ cup liquid)
1 can (16 ounces) Chinese
    vegetables, drained
1 can (16 ounces) bean sprouts,
    rinsed and drained
½ teaspoon salt

Cut meat into ½-inch slices, then cut slices into ¼-inch strips. Use large skillet with non-stick finish or coat regular skillet with vegetable spray-on for cookware. Cook and stir meat in skillet until brown. Stir in celery, onion, soy sauce, monosodium glutamate, bouillon and water. Cover and simmer 30 minutes.

Mix cornstarch and reserved mushroom liquid; stir into meat mixture. Stir in mushrooms and Chinese vegetables. Cook, stirring constantly, until mixture thickens and boils. Boil and stir 1 minute.

Sprinkle bean sprouts with salt and heat, stirring occasionally. Serve meat mixture on bean sprouts.

6 servings/200 calories each. (Each serving: scant 1 cup meat mixture, ⅓ cup bean sprouts.)

BRAISED PORK TENDERLOIN PATTIES

4 pork tenderloin patties (about
    4 ounces each), ½ inch thick
2 teaspoons soy sauce
Garlic salt
1 to 2 tablespoons water

Use large skillet with non-stick finish or coat regular skillet with vegetable spray-on for cookware. Place patties in skillet; sprinkle each with ¼ teaspoon soy sauce and dash garlic salt and brown over medium-high heat. Turn; sprinkle each patty with ¼ teaspoon soy sauce and dash garlic salt and brown other side. Add water to skillet; cover and cook over low heat until patties are done, about 30 minutes. Serve meat with pan juices.

4 servings/215 calories each.

SUPER SUPPER SALAD

1 can (16 ounces) sauerkraut,
    drained (reserve liquid)
1 Bermuda onion, thinly sliced
2 dill pickles, cut into julienne
    strips
1 tart apple, pared and sliced
1⅓ cups diced cooked ham (about
    ½ pound)

In salad bowl, layer ⅓ each sauerkraut, onion slices, dill pickle strips, apple slices and meat. Repeat 2 times. Drizzle reserved sauerkraut liquid on top. Cover and refrigerate about 1 hour.

4 servings/105 calories each. (Each serving: 1 cup.)

385-Calorie Dinner—Rosy Consommé (page 64), San Francisco Chicken Salad (page 20), Broccoli Spears (¾ cup) with Butter (1 teaspoon), Triangle Crackers, Rocky Road Cheese-Fruit Whip (page 52).

395-Calorie Dinner—Company Fish Roulades (page 23), Sea Breeze Tossed Potato Salad (page 31), Carrot Sticks, Lacy Melba Toast (page 63), Melon (⅛) with Grapes (⅓ cup), Skim Milk (1 cup).

VEAL CHARLOTTE

6 veal cutlets (4 ounces each) or
  1½-pound veal round steak
2 teaspoons instant beef bouillon
½ teaspoon paprika
1 pound mushrooms, sliced
½ teaspoon salt
¼ teaspoon garlic powder
1 teaspoon grated lemon peel
1 tablespoon lemon juice
⅓ cup water
2 teaspoons cornstarch
1 teaspoon instant beef bouillon
⅛ teaspoon salt
1 cup water
Poppy Seed Noodles (right)
Lemon wedges
Parsley

Use large skillet with non-stick finish or coat regular skillet with vegetable spray-on for cookware. If using veal round steak, cut into 6 pieces and pound until each piece is ¼ inch thick. Sprinkle meat with 2 teaspoons bouillon and the paprika; brown in skillet over medium-high heat. Arrange mushrooms on meat. Mix ½ teaspoon salt, the garlic powder, lemon peel, lemon juice and ⅓ cup water; pour over mushrooms. Reduce heat; cover and simmer until meat is done, about 30 minutes. (If necessary, add small amount of water.)

Mix cornstarch, 1 teaspoon bouillon, ⅛ teaspoon salt and 1 cup water; stir into meat mixture. Heat to boiling, stirring constantly. Boil and stir 1 minute. Serve meat mixture on Poppy Seed Noodles and garnish with lemon wedges and parsley.

6 servings/310 calories each. (Each serving: meat, ⅓ cup mushrooms, 2 tablespoons gravy, ½ cup noodles.)

Poppy Seed Noodles
Heat 6 cups water and 1 tablespoon salt to boiling. Add 8 ounces medium noodles (4 to 5 cups); heat to boiling. Boil uncovered, stirring occasionally, 7 to 10 minutes; drain. Toss noodles with 2 teaspoons poppy seed.

PEPPER CHICKEN

2½- to 3-pound broiler-fryer
  chicken, cut up
¼ cup soy sauce
1 tablespoon water
½ teaspoon garlic powder
1 can (8½ ounces) water
  chestnuts, drained and sliced
1 green pepper, cut into 1-inch
  pieces
2 teaspoons cornstarch
2 tablespoons water

Remove skin and fat from chicken. Place chicken in large skillet. Mix soy sauce, 1 tablespoon water and the garlic powder; pour over chicken. Cover and refrigerate 1 hour, turning chicken once.

Heat to boiling; reduce heat and simmer 40 minutes. Scatter water chestnut slices and green pepper pieces on chicken; cover and simmer until chicken is tender, 15 to 20 minutes.

Mix cornstarch and 2 tablespoons water; stir into liquid in skillet. Cook, stirring constantly, until mixture thickens and boils. Boil and stir 1 minute.

6 servings/190 calories each.

CHICKEN WITH MUSHROOM GRAVY

Double savings: Skinning the chicken subtracts 70 calories for three ounces of bird; non-stick, non-fat cooking reduces the count even more.

  6 chicken breast halves (3 pounds)
  1 cup tomato juice
  1 can (4 ounces) mushroom stems and pieces, drained (reserve liquid)
  ⅓ cup finely chopped onion
  1 tablespoon parsley flakes
1½ teaspoons salt
  1 teaspoon basil leaves
  ⅛ teaspoon garlic powder
  2 teaspoons cornstarch
  2 tablespoons water

Remove skin from chicken. Use large skillet with non-stick finish or coat regular skillet with vegetable spray-on for cookware. Heat skillet; brown chicken over medium-high heat. Pour tomato juice and reserved mushroom liquid onto chicken. Stir in onion, parsley flakes, salt, basil leaves and garlic powder. Cover and simmer until chicken is tender, 50 to 60 minutes. Stir in mushrooms.

Mix cornstarch and water; stir into liquid in skillet. Cook, stirring constantly, until mixture thickens and boils. Boil and stir 1 minute.

6 servings/230 calories each.

SAN FRANCISCO CHICKEN SALAD

A salad-supper—perfect warm-weather strategy. Pictured on page 17.

  3 chicken breast halves (about 1½ pounds)
  ½ teaspoon crushed gingerroot or ¼ teaspoon ground ginger
  ½ teaspoon salt
  1 medium head lettuce
  3 green onions, cut into thin strips
  2 tomatoes, cut into wedges
  ¼ cup toasted sesame seed*
Oil-and-Vinegar Dressing (below)

Remove skin from chicken. Place chicken in large saucepan; add enough water to cover. Add gingerroot and salt; heat to boiling. Reduce heat; cover and simmer until chicken is tender, 30 to 40 minutes. Remove from heat; cool chicken in broth.

Remove meat from bones; cut meat into 1-inch pieces (about 3 cups). Into large bowl, tear lettuce into bite-size pieces. Add chicken, onions, tomatoes, sesame seed and dressing; toss.

6 servings/155 calories each. (Each serving: 1½ cups.)

*To toast sesame seed, spread on ungreased baking sheet and bake in 350° oven, stirring occasionally, until golden, 10 to 15 minutes.

Oil-and-Vinegar Dressing
  1 tablespoon sugar
  2 tablespoons vinegar
  1 tablespoon salad oil
1½ teaspoons salt
  1 teaspoon monosodium glutamate
  ½ teaspoon pepper

Shake all ingredients in tightly covered jar.

TURKEY MEATBALLS MANDARIN

1 pound ground turkey
1 teaspoon salt
1 teaspoon instant minced onion
¼ teaspoon garlic powder
1 tablespoon chopped pimiento
1 tablespoon soy sauce
1 egg
4 cups water
1 teaspoon salt
2 tablespoons soy sauce
½ teaspoon crushed gingerroot or
   ¼ teaspoon ground ginger
1 package (7 ounces) frozen
   Chinese pea pods
1 teaspoon cornstarch
1 tablespoon water
3 cups Hot Cooked Rice (page 11)
Parsley
1 can (11 ounces) mandarin orange
   segments, drained

Mix meat, 1 teaspoon salt, the onion, garlic powder, pimiento, 1 tablespoon soy sauce and the egg thoroughly. Shape mixture into 1½-inch balls.

In large skillet, heat 4 cups water, 1 teaspoon salt, 2 tablespoons soy sauce and the gingerroot to boiling. Place meatballs in seasoned water; heat to boiling. Reduce heat; cover and simmer until meatballs are done, about 30 minutes. While meatballs simmer, cook pea pods as directed on package; drain.

With slotted spoon, remove meatballs to warm platter. Strain liquid; reserve 1 cup. Mix cornstarch and 1 tablespoon water in same skillet. Stir in reserved liquid. Cook, stirring constantly, until mixture thickens and boils. Boil and stir 1 minute.

Arrange meatballs on rice. Arrange pea pods around meatballs; garnish with parsley and orange segments. Serve with gravy.

6 servings/250 calories each. (Each serving: 3 meatballs, ½ cup rice, pea pods and orange segments, 2 tablespoons gravy.)

Variation

Beef Meatballs Mandarin: Substitute 1 pound lean ground beef for the ground turkey; decrease salt in meat mixture to ¾ teaspoon. (6 servings/260 calories each. Each serving: 3 meatballs, ½ cup rice, pea pods and orange segments, 2 tablespoons gravy.)

Sobering thought: One hundred extra calories a day—1 tablespoon of butter or a 2-inch biscuit or a scoop of ice milk—can add up to 10 extra pounds in a year.

SAUCY TURKEY ROLL

A cup of this cut-up turkey without fatty skin comes to just 265 calories. Mix with Mock Mayonnaise (page 40) for a nice chunky salad—or slice the turkey for sandwiches.

2- to 2½-pound turkey roast*
   (without gravy)
½ cup rosé
1 tablespoon soy sauce
½ teaspoon rosemary leaves
½ teaspoon marjoram leaves

Bake turkey roast as directed on package except—before baking, mix remaining ingredients and pour onto roast. Cut roast into ½-inch slices and spoon 1 tablespoon pan juice on each slice.

About 10 slices/95 calories each.

NOTE: For 3½- to 4-pound turkey roast, bake in ungreased baking pan, 11 x 7 x 1½ inches, and double the amounts of remaining ingredients. Cut roast into ½-inch slices and spoon 1 tablespoon pan juice on each slice. (About 14 slices/95 calories each.)

*If turkey roast is in cello-bag and directions call for baking in bag, do not remove. Snip X with kitchen scissors in top of bag; pour remaining ingredients through funnel into bag.

For one of your daily cereal or bread servings, try rice or noodles for a nice change of pace. Just be extra careful in measuring your portion.

TURKEY BURGERS

Turkey and cranberry sauce in unexpected burgers. Store ground turkey in the coldest part of the refrigerator and use within 24 hours, or freeze for future use.

1 pound ground turkey
1 teaspoon salt
¼ teaspoon sage
2 tablespoons finely chopped
   onion
¼ cup jellied cranberry sauce
¼ teaspoon horseradish
¼ cup water
1 drop red food color (optional)

Use large skillet with non-stick finish or coat regular skillet with vegetable spray-on for cookware. Mix meat, salt, sage and onion. Shape mixture into 4 patties, about 3½ inches in diameter and ¾ inch thick. Cook in skillet over medium heat, turning frequently, until light brown and done, about 15 minutes.

While patties cook, heat remaining ingredients until hot, stirring occasionally. Spoon 2 tablespoons cranberry mixture onto each patty.

4 servings/255 calories each.

COMPANY FISH ROULADES

Deliciously different dinner-party fare for the calorie-conscious. Pictured on page 18.

2 pounds frozen fish fillets
   (skinless), thawed
2 tablespoons lemon juice
Paprika
Salt and pepper
About 8 large dill pickles, cut crosswise
   into 1-inch pieces
16 lemon slices
⅓ cup chili sauce
2 packages (10 ounces each)
   frozen chopped spinach

Heat oven to 350°. Cut fish fillets into strips 1 inch wide and long enough to wrap around pickle pieces. Sprinkle both sides of fish strips with lemon juice, paprika, salt and pepper. Roll a fish strip around each pickle piece; secure with wooden picks. Place fish rolls upright on ungreased rack in broiler pan. Top each with a lemon slice and 1 teaspoon chili sauce. Bake until fish flakes easily with a fork, 20 to 25 minutes.

While fish roulades are baking, cook spinach as directed on package; drain. Turn into serving dish; place hot fish roulades on top.

8 servings/155 calories each. (Each serving: 2 roulades, about ⅓ cup spinach.)

FLOUNDER VINAIGRETTE

2 packages (16 ounces each)
   frozen flounder fillets (skinless)
Paprika
Salt
Six 1½-inch-thick tomato slices
1 tablespoon snipped chives
½ teaspoon tarragon leaves
½ cup low-calorie Italian dressing
¼ cup shredded Cheddar cheese
1 tablespoon snipped parsley

Heat oven to 475°. Use baking pan, 13 x 9 x 2 inches, with non-stick finish or coat regular baking pan with vegetable spray-on for cookware. Cut each frozen block of fish into 3 pieces. (Let fish stand at room temperature 10 minutes before cutting.)

Arrange fish in baking pan. Sprinkle with paprika and salt. Place a tomato slice on each serving; sprinkle with salt, chives and tarragon leaves. Pour dressing on fish and top each serving with 2 teaspoons cheese. Bake uncovered until fish flakes easily with a fork, 20 to 25 minutes. Sprinkle parsley on each serving.

6 servings/145 calories each.

Poke a hole in the end of a lemon with a wooden pick—now you have a super squirter for fish, salads or vegetables.

BROILED SOY HALIBUT STEAKS

Crusty and flaky, with an elusive whisper of garlic. This recipe's just as good with salmon steaks.

2 pounds halibut steaks (about 6)
3 tablespoons soy sauce
1 teaspoon ginger
½ teaspoon garlic powder
1 teaspoon grated lemon peel
¼ cup lemon juice
¼ cup water
Lemon slices
Parsley

Place fish in ungreased baking dish, 13½ x 9 x 2 inches. Mix remaining ingredients except lemon slices and parsley; pour onto fish. Cover and refrigerate at least 8 hours.

Set oven control at broil and/or 550°. Drain fish; reserve marinade. Place fish on greased rack in broiler pan. Brushing fish occasionally with reserved marinade, broil with top 4 inches from heat 5 to 7 minutes on each side. Garnish with lemon slices and parsley.

6 servings/160 calories each.

Dish up servings in the kitchen instead of from platters and vegetable dishes at the table. That way you can give yourself exact measured amounts. (Handy device: a #8 ice-cream scoop measures ½ cup—of anything.)

DILLED FISH STICKS

A double dill delight. Fish sticks flavored with dill marinade and garnished with dill pickle slices.

1 package (16 ounces) frozen pike or flounder fillets (skinless)
1 teaspoon salt
½ teaspoon dill weed
2 drops red pepper sauce
⅓ cup unsweetened grapefruit juice
½ teaspoon paprika
2 teaspoons finely chopped onion
Six ¼-inch-thick lengthwise slices dill pickle
Sprigs of dill or parsley

Cut frozen block of fish into 6 sticks. (To make this easier, let fish stand at room temperature 10 minutes before cutting.)

Arrange fish in ungreased baking pan, 13 x 9 x 2 inches. Mix salt, dill weed, red pepper sauce and grapefruit juice; pour over fish. Let stand at room temperature 1 hour, turning fish frequently.

Heat oven to 475°. Sprinkle fish with paprika, then top each piece with onion and a dill pickle slice. Bake uncovered until fish flakes easily with a fork, about 15 minutes. Garnish with sprigs of dill.

3 servings/120 calories each. (Each serving: 2 sticks.)

PARTY SHRIMP ORIENTAL

 1 pound cleaned raw shrimp,
   fresh or frozen (about 2 cups)
 2 tablespoons soy sauce
 1 tablespoon sherry
 1 teaspoon crushed gingerroot or
   ½ teaspoon ground ginger
 ¼ teaspoon salt
1½ cups sliced onion
 1 cup ¼-inch diagonal slices
   celery
 1 can (8½ ounces) water
   chestnuts, drained and sliced
 1 can (16 ounces) bean sprouts,
   rinsed and drained
 1 tablespoon cornstarch
 ½ teaspoon instant chicken
   bouillon
 ½ cup water
 6 slices Lacy Melba Toast
   (page 63)

In large skillet, cook and stir shrimp, soy sauce, sherry, gingerroot and salt over high heat until shrimp are pink, about 6 minutes. Remove shrimp and set aside.

In same skillet, cook and stir onion, celery, water chestnuts and bean sprouts until celery is crisp-tender, about 6 minutes. Stir in shrimp. Mix cornstarch, bouillon and water. Stir into shrimp mixture. Cook, stirring constantly, until mixture thickens and boils. Boil and stir 1 minute. Serve shrimp mixture over toast.

6 servings/165 calories each. (Each serving: scant 1 cup shrimp mixture, 1 slice toast.)

FAST FISH CHOWDER

 1 pound fresh or frozen pike,
   pollock or halibut fillets
 3 cups tomato juice
 1 medium onion, sliced
 3 lemon slices
 1 bay leaf
 ½ teaspoon salt
 2 peppercorns
Snipped parsley

Thaw fish if frozen. Cut fish into bite-size pieces. In large saucepan, heat remaining ingredients except parsley to boiling. Add fish; heat to boiling. Reduce heat; cover and simmer until fish flakes easily with a fork, 4 to 6 minutes. Serve in soup bowls and sprinkle each serving with parsley.

5 servings/125 calories. (Each serving: 1 cup.)

Get into action. Set a time to exercise regularly—then make it a must till it turns into a habit.

SALMON-CITRUS SALAD

1 carton (8 ounces) unflavored yogurt (1 cup)
1 tablespoon grated grapefruit peel
½ teaspoon salt
3 cups bite-size pieces spinach (about 3 ounces)
1 cup thin diagonal slices celery
1 can (16 ounces) salmon, cleaned, drained and broken into pieces
1 grapefruit, pared and sectioned
1 teaspoon seasoned salt
1 tablespoon tarragon vinegar
Romaine leaves
Paprika

Mix yogurt, grapefruit peel and salt in small bowl; cover and refrigerate until serving time.

Toss remaining ingredients except romaine leaves and paprika. Turn salad into bowl lined with romaine leaves; sprinkle with paprika. Serve with yogurt dressing.

6 servings/145 calories each. (Each serving: 1 cup.)

Don't let a lapse throw you. If you do go over your calorie count, resolve to start over at the next meal. Think success!

TUNA PINEAPPLE BOATS

1 pineapple
2 cans (7 ounces each) white tuna in water, drained and broken into chunks
1 cup strawberries (reserve 4 whole berries for garnish), sliced
2 cups cantaloupe or honeydew melon balls
¼ teaspoon ginger
2 tablespoons lime juice
2 tablespoons coarsely chopped dry roasted almonds
Dash ginger
Pineapple yogurt

Select a pineapple with fresh green leaves. Cut pineapple lengthwise into quarters through green top. Cut along the curved edges of quarters with grapefruit knife to remove fruit. Cut fruit into chunks; remove core. Drain fruit and invert shells to drain.

Place pineapple chunks, tuna, sliced strawberries and melon balls in large bowl. Sprinkle with ¼ teaspoon ginger and the lime juice and toss. Cover and refrigerate 1 hour.

Spoon pineapple mixture into shells; sprinkle with almonds and dash ginger. Spoon 1 tablespoon yogurt onto each serving and garnish with reserved whole strawberries.

4 servings/255 calories each.

QUICHE FRANÇAISE

Food for thought: If this quiche were baked in a pie shell, it would cost upwards of a thousand calories more. The rice crust saves about 145 calories a serving.

1½ cups hot cooked regular rice
1 tablespoon snipped chives
1 egg white
1 package (3 ounces) sliced smoked beef
3 eggs plus 1 egg yolk
1 can (13 ounces) evaporated skim milk
¼ teaspoon salt
½ cup shredded mozzarella or Monterey (Jack) cheese
2 tablespoons instant minced onion
8 tomato slices

Heat oven to 350°. Use 10-inch pie pan with non-stick finish or coat regular pie pan with vegetable spray-on for cookware. Beat rice, chives and egg white with fork. Turn mixture into pie pan; spread evenly with rubber scraper on bottom and halfway up side of pie pan. (Do not leave any holes.) Bake 5 minutes.

Tear meat into small pieces and sprinkle in rice crust. Beat eggs, egg yolk, skim milk and salt thoroughly; stir in cheese and onion. Carefully pour into rice crust. Bake until knife inserted 1 inch from edge comes out clean, 25 to 30 minutes. Immediately run knife around edge to loosen crust. Let quiche stand 10 minutes before serving. Cut into wedges; top each wedge with a tomato slice.

8 servings/190 calories each.

CHINESE QUICHE

1 cup hot cooked regular rice
1 teaspoon soy sauce
¼ teaspoon ginger
1 egg white
2 eggs plus 1 egg yolk
1 cup skim milk
¾ teaspoon salt
½ can (16-ounce size) Chinese vegetables, drained (1 cup)
1 cup cut-up cooked chicken
2 green onions, sliced (with tops)
Pimiento strips
Spicy Soy Sauce (below)

Heat oven to 350°. Use 9-inch pie pan with non-stick finish or coat regular pie pan with vegetable spray-on for cookware. Beat rice, soy sauce, ginger and egg white with fork. Turn mixture into pie pan; spread evenly with rubber scraper on bottom and halfway up side of pie pan. (Do not leave any holes.)

Beat eggs, egg yolk, milk and salt thoroughly; stir in vegetables, chicken and onions. Carefully pour into rice crust. Bake until knife inserted 1 inch from edge comes out clean, 30 to 40 minutes. Immediately run knife around edge to loosen crust. Let quiche stand 10 minutes before serving. Cut into wedges; garnish with pimiento strips and serve with Spicy Soy Sauce.

8 servings/135 calories each.

Spicy Soy Sauce
Mix 3 tablespoons soy sauce, ½ cup water and ⅛ teaspoon ginger.

BAKED EGG WITH BROCCOLI

Heat oven to 325°. For each serving, coat a 6-ounce custard cup with vegetable spray-on for cookware. Place 2 tablespoons cooked chopped broccoli in cup; season with garlic salt. Carefully break an egg into cup; season with salt. Sprinkle 1 tablespoon shredded Cheddar cheese on top of egg. Bake uncovered until egg is desired consistency, 15 to 18 minutes. Serve in custard cup or unmold.

1 serving/110 calories.

Be a con artist. Arrange foods attractively to fill your plate. Use smaller-size dishes, spread food out and conceal any gaps with vegetable snacks (page 35), celery leaves or parsley.

OVEN OMELET WITH SPINACH

Fluffy main-dish delight. Golden brown with cheese and tomatoes on top, it's a satisfying supper. Serve with Tangy Mushroom Salad (page 30) on the side and fresh fruit for dessert.

1 package (10 ounces) frozen chopped spinach
9 eggs
2 tablespoons instant minced onion
2 tablespoons skim milk
1 teaspoon salt
½ teaspoon basil leaves
¼ teaspoon garlic powder
8 peeled tomato slices
½ cup shredded mozzarella cheese

Heat oven to 325°. Use baking pan, 11 x 7 x 1½ inches, with non-stick finish or coat regular pan with vegetable spray-on for cookware. Cook spinach as directed on package; drain.

Beat eggs until light and fluffy. Stir in spinach, onion, skim milk, salt, basil leaves and garlic powder. Pour into pan. Arrange tomato slices on top and sprinkle with cheese. Bake uncovered until set, 25 to 30 minutes.

8 servings/135 calories each.

SALADS AND VEGETABLES — YOUR BIGGEST BREAKS

Or
How to Fill Up with Fewer Calories

Greens are great—colorful, crisp and practically scot-free of calories. To add zip to them, toss in crunchy raw vegetables or naturally sweet, tangy fruits and low-calorie dressings. Along with salads, serve cooked vegetables—hot, filling and superbly seasoned with herbs and spices instead of butter and rich sauces. Together, salads and vegetables make up a very important part of your nutritional needs. And you get so much for the calories spent!

TANGY MUSHROOM SALAD

For each serving, tear Bibb or Boston lettuce into bite-size pieces (¾ cup) into salad bowl. Add ¼ cup sliced fresh mushrooms and 1 tablespoon Make-your-own Cocktail Sauce (below) and toss.

1 serving/35 calories.

Make-your-own Cocktail Sauce
1 bottle (12 ounces) chili sauce
1 tablespoon horseradish
1 tablespoon lemon juice
½ teaspoon Worcestershire sauce
¼ teaspoon salt
Dash pepper

Mix all ingredients. Refrigerate leftover sauce. (About 1½ cups/15 calories per tablespoon.)

Variation
Tangy Shrimp Appetizer Salad: Add ¼ cup cleaned cooked shrimp with the mushrooms. (1 serving/75 calories.)

Bulky foods that fill you up: a mound of green vegetables, a giant salad with low-calorie dressing or a big bowl of ready-to-eat unsweetened cereal.

SPINACH-SPROUT SALAD

A crunchy, colorful salad—perfect with beef or chicken. And the subtly flavored dressing sets it off just right.

---

8 ounces spinach or curly endive
1 can (16 ounces) bean sprouts,
    rinsed and drained
1 can (8½ ounces) water chestnuts,
    drained and sliced
Sesame Dressing (below)
1 cup croutons (optional)

Tear spinach into bite-size pieces into salad bowl. Add bean sprouts, water chestnuts and dressing and toss. Sprinkle croutons on top.

8 servings/25 calories each without croutons; 65 calories each with croutons. (Each serving: ¾ cup.)

Sesame Dressing
¼ cup soy sauce
2 tablespoons toasted sesame
    seed*
2 tablespoons lemon juice
1 tablespoon finely chopped onion
½ teaspoon sugar
¼ teaspoon pepper

Mix all ingredients.

*To toast sesame seed, spread on ungreased baking sheet and bake in 350° oven, stirring occasionally, until golden, 10 to 15 minutes.

TOSSED SALAD ITALIANO

For a fancier presentation, line a platter with greens, arrange the vegetables separately on it, put dressing in a cruet. Presto! A colorful salad buffet.

1 package (9 ounces) frozen Italian green beans, cooked, drained and cooled
1 pound small zucchini (about 4), cut into ¼-inch slices
1 small onion, thinly sliced
1 cup cherry tomatoes, cut into halves
¼ teaspoon garlic salt
½ cup low-calorie Italian dressing
2 tablespoons shredded mozzarella cheese

Combine vegetables in bowl and sprinkle with garlic salt. Pour dressing over vegetables and toss. Sprinkle cheese on top.

6 servings/50 calories each. (Each serving: ⅔ cup.)

WINTER TOMATO SALAD

1 small cauliflower, separated into flowerets
1 can (16 ounces) tomato wedges, drained
½ cup chopped onion
1 tablespoon vinegar
1 teaspoon seasoned salt
¼ teaspoon pepper
6 lettuce cups

Toss all ingredients except lettuce cups in bowl. Cover and refrigerate at least 30 minutes.

With slotted spoon, remove vegetables to lettuce cups.

6 servings/35 calories each. (Each serving: ¾ cup.)

SEA BREEZE TOSSED POTATO SALAD

A real potato-lover's calorie bargain. In a hurry? Use little canned potatoes. Pictured on page 18.

½ cup low-calorie Italian dressing
2 cups hot cubed cooked potatoes
1 small cucumber
4 hard-cooked eggs, each cut into 4 wedges
1 cup ½-inch diagonal slices celery
½ teaspoon seasoned salt
1 tablespoon dill weed
3 cups bite-size pieces lettuce
2 tablespoons snipped parsley

Pour dressing over potatoes in large bowl; cover and refrigerate 1 hour.

Thinly slice unpared cucumber into bowl; add remaining ingredients except parsley and toss. Sprinkle parsley on top.

8 servings/75 calories each. (Each serving: ¾ cup.)

When you're lunching solo: Sit down. Eat slowly. After every third bite put your fork down and pause. You'll find that the more time you take to eat, the less food it takes to satisfy you.

MEXICAN SALAD

1 small head lettuce
2 large oranges, pared and sectioned, or 1 can (11 ounces) mandarin orange segments, drained
1 cucumber, scored and sliced
1 small onion, thinly sliced and separated into rings
2 tablespoons chopped red chilies or pimiento
½ teaspoon chili powder
Chili Dressing (below)

Coarsely shred lettuce. Toss lettuce and remaining ingredients except Chili Dressing in bowl. Spoon 1 tablespoon dressing onto each serving.

8 servings/40 calories each. (Each serving: ¾ cup.)

Chili Dressing
Mix 1 carton (8 ounces) unflavored yogurt (1 cup), 1 tablespoon chili sauce and 1 teaspoon onion salt. (1 cup/10 calories per tablespoon.)

About dressing. Our salad recipes call for specific amounts of dressing; they're included in the calorie count for the salad. To help you figure extra-helping costs, calories are given for individual dressings.

CONSOMME VEGETABLE WREATH

True party fare, an eye-catcher on a buffet table with ham or beef. And only you will know that a generous serving, complete with dressing, is a mere 40 calories.

---

1 can (10½ ounces) condensed consommé (beef gelatin added)
1 cup water
¼ teaspoon garlic salt
1 tablespoon Worcestershire sauce
1 envelope unflavored gelatin
1 cup uncooked cauliflowerets
1 cup small cherry tomatoes
Yogurt Dressing (below)

Combine consommé, water, garlic salt and Worcestershire sauce in small saucepan. Sprinkle gelatin on liquid to soften. Stir over medium heat until gelatin is dissolved, about 3 minutes. Refrigerate until slightly thickened but not set.

Pour about ⅓ of gelatin mixture into 5-cup ring mold. Arrange vegetables in gelatin. Pour remaining gelatin mixture on vegetables. Refrigerate until set, about 4 hours.

Unmold onto serving plate. Cut into 6 servings. Spoon 2 tablespoons Yogurt Dressing on each serving.

6 servings/40 calories each. (Each serving: ¾ cup.)

Yogurt Dressing
Mix 1 carton (8 ounces) unflavored yogurt (1 cup), 1 teaspoon horseradish, ½ teaspoon salt and ¼ teaspoon garlic salt.

CANTALOUPE MOLD WITH TEAHOUSE TOPPING

A colorful salad that's ideal for do-aheaders. Pictured on page 36.

1 cup boiling water
1 envelope low-calorie
   orange-flavored gelatin
¾ cup unsweetened orange juice
¼ teaspoon ginger
2 cups small melon balls
   (cantaloupe and/or honeydew)
Teahouse Topping (below)

Pour boiling water on gelatin in bowl; stir until gelatin is dissolved. Stir in orange juice and ginger. Refrigerate until slightly thickened but not set.

Stir in melon balls. Pour into a 4-cup mold or 6 individual molds. Refrigerate until set, about 4 hours. Unmold onto serving plate. Spoon 1 generous tablespoon Teahouse Topping onto each serving.

6 servings/60 calories each. (Each serving: ⅔ cup.)

Teahouse Topping
Mix ½ cup frozen whipped topping (thawed) and 1 teaspoon instant tea.

GAZPACHO MOLD

Sophisticated Mexican cold soup turned into a molded salad. Recommended for adult tastes only.

2 cups vegetable juice cocktail
2 teaspoons instant beef bouillon
2 envelopes unflavored gelatin
2 to 3 tablespoons wine vinegar
2 tomatoes, peeled and coarsely
   chopped
1 small cucumber, cut into ¼-inch
   cubes
2 teaspoons instant minced onion
¾ teaspoon salt
6 drops red pepper sauce
Leaf lettuce

Combine vegetable juice cocktail and bouillon in medium saucepan. Sprinkle gelatin on liquid to soften. Stir over medium heat until gelatin is dissolved, about 3 minutes. Stir in vinegar. Refrigerate until slightly thickened but not set.

Stir in tomatoes, cucumber, onion, salt and red pepper sauce. Pour into baking pan, 8 x 8 x 2 inches, or 5-cup ring mold. Refrigerate until set, about 4 hours. Unmold onto lettuce.

9 servings/30 calories each. (Each serving: about ¾ cup.)

PICKLED ARTICHOKES

1 can (14 ounces) artichoke hearts, drained (reserve liquid)
2 tablespoons instant minced onion
3 tablespoons dry sherry (optional)
2 tablespoon soy sauce
¼ cup vinegar
1 teaspoon salt

Place artichokes in 1-quart standard jar. Heat reserved artichoke liquid and remaining ingredients to boiling; pour into jar. Cover and refrigerate 24 hours. Drain; serve artichokes in salad or as a relish.

4 servings/30 calories each without sherry; 45 calories each with sherry. (Each serving: ½ cup.)

Cool it. If you're tempted to nibble as you cook, keep a glass of ice water at hand and sip instead of tasting.

PICKLED MUSHROOMS

36 small mushroom caps or 16 large mushrooms, cut into halves
¼ cup vinegar
3 tablespoons dry sherry (optional)
2 tablespoons soy sauce
1 teaspoon salt
½ small onion, sliced and separated into rings

Place mushrooms in 1-quart standard jar. Heat remaining ingredients to boiling; pour into jar. Cover and refrigerate at least 24 hours. Drain; serve mushrooms and onions in salad or as a relish.

4 servings/40 calories each without sherry; 55 calories each with sherry. (Each serving: ½ cup.)

PICKLED CUCUMBERS

1 cucumber
½ medium onion, thinly sliced and separated into rings
½ cup vinegar
½ cup water
¼ teaspoon salt
Dash pepper

Run tines of fork lengthwise on unpared cucumber. Thinly slice cucumber into bowl. Add onion rings. Mix remaining ingredients; pour onto vegetables. Cover and refrigerate at least 1 hour. Drain before serving.

4 servings/15 calories each. (Each serving: about ½ cup.)

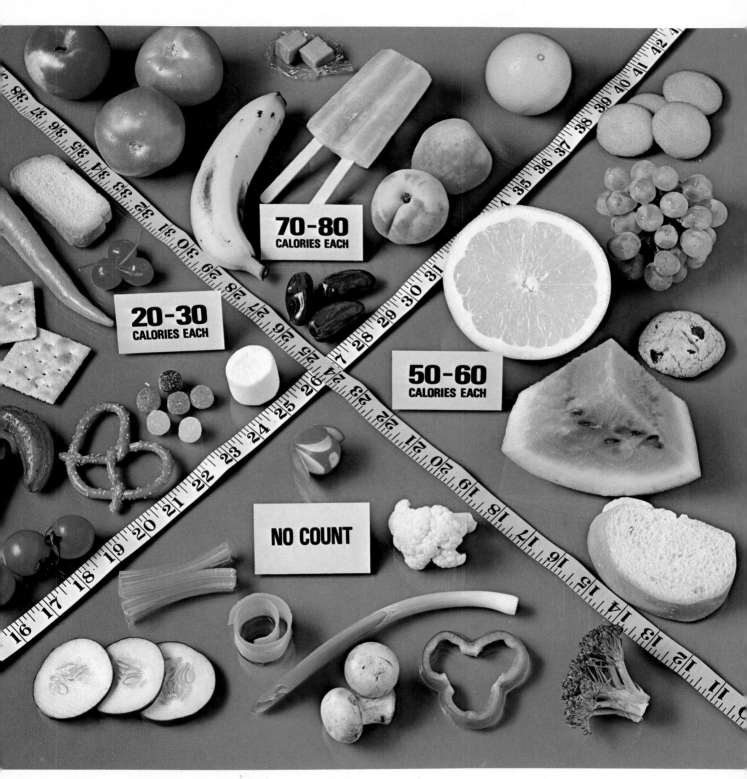

70-80 CALORIES EACH

20-30 CALORIES EACH

50-60 CALORIES EACH

NO COUNT

Snacks—For specific calories for items or groups of items pictured, see pages 68–70.

405-Calorie Dinner—Pork Chow Mein (page 16), Cantaloupe Mold with Teahouse Topping (page 33), Rice (⅓ cup), Homemade Lime Sherbet (page 57).

395-Calorie Dinner—No-Noodle Lasagne (page 13), Orange-Onion Salad (¾ cup) with Cucumber Dressing (page 40, 1 tablespoon), Bread Stick (4-inch), Spoon-up Eggnog (page 57).

4
lunches under
300
calories

Four Lunches Under 300 Calories (at right).

FOUR LUNCHES UNDER 300 CALORIES

Spring Fever Soup 'n Sandwich/280 calories
Quick Spinach Soup (page 65)
Open-face Chicken Sandwich (page 63)
Strawberries (½ cup), Sugar (2 teaspoons)
Skim Milk (1 cup)

Summer Fruit 'n Ham Plate/280 calories
Lean Ham Slices (2 ounces) on Leaf Lettuce
Cantaloupe (¼ melon, 5 inches in diameter)
with Blueberries (½ cup)
Lacy Melba Toast (page 63)
Neufchâtel Cheese (½ ounce)
Iced Tea

Autumn Broiler Lunch/295 calories
Bean Sprout Burger (page 12)
Thin Toasted Bun Slice (¼ bun)
Mushroom Topper (page 43)
Broccoli Flowerets, Broiled Tomato Half
Celery Stalk
Root Beer in the Clouds (page 60)

Winter Salad-Sandwich Plate/250 calories
Tangy Shrimp Appetizer Salad (page 30)
Crunchy Cottage Cheese (page 63) on Rye
Beans (½ cup), Carrots, Olives
Broiled Grapefruit

SALAD DRESSINGS

Cucumber Dressing
 ½ cup chopped cucumber
 1½ teaspoons instant minced
      onion
 1 teaspoon horseradish
 ½ teaspoon salt
 1 carton (8 ounces) unflavored
      yogurt (1 cup)

Beat all ingredients with rotary beater. Refrigerate leftover dressing.

1¼ cups/10 calories per tablespoon.

Curry-Caper Dressing or Dip
 1 carton (8 ounces) unflavored
      yogurt (1 cup)
 ¼ cup mayonnaise or salad dressing
 ¼ teaspoon salt
 ¼ teaspoon curry powder
 ⅛ teaspoon garlic powder
 ½ teaspoon instant beef bouillon
 2 tablespoons capers, drained

Measure all ingredients into blender. Cover and blend on medium speed 10 seconds. Scrape sides with rubber spatula; blend 10 seconds longer. Refrigerate leftover dressing.

2½ cups/20 calories per tablespoon.

Take a reading on all the low-calorie salad dressings that now come bottled. And while you're at it, compare the counts—they vary quite a bit.

Creamy Orange Dressing
Shake 1 can (13 ounces) evaporated skim milk and 1 can (6 ounces) frozen orange juice concentrate (thawed) in tightly covered jar. Refrigerate leftover dressing.

2 cups/20 calories per tablespoon.

Fluffy Fruit Dressing
Beat 1 carton (8 ounces) unflavored yogurt (1 cup) and 3 tablespoons raspberry or strawberry jam or orange marmalade with rotary beater. Refrigerate leftover dressing.

1 cup/20 calories per tablespoon.

Mock Mayonnaise
 1 carton (8 ounces) unflavored
      yogurt (1 cup)
 2 tablespoons mayonnaise
 ¼ teaspoon salt
Dash paprika
 1 drop yellow food color

Mix all ingredients with rotary beater until smooth. Cover and refrigerate 2 hours before serving.

About 1 cup/20 calories per tablespoon.

EASY BAKED ASPARAGUS

Heat oven to 325°. Break off tough ends of 1 pound asparagus as far down as stalks snap easily. Place stalks in single layer in ungreased baking pan, 8 x 8 x 2 inches. Sprinkle with ½ teaspoon seasoned salt, ½ teaspoon salt and 1 tablespoon water. Cover tightly with aluminum foil and bake until tender, 20 to 30 minutes.

4 servings/30 calories each.

JAPANESE-STYLE CABBAGE

Actual cooking for this recipe takes just about five minutes. You can chop the cabbage ahead of time, and while you're at it, chop some extra and snack on it freely—only 20 calories for a whole cup.

½ cup chicken broth
2 tablespoons soy sauce
4 cups thinly sliced cabbage
1 cup sliced celery
1 tablespoon chopped green onion

In large skillet, heat chicken broth and soy sauce to boiling. Stir in cabbage, celery and onion. Cook over high heat, turning vegetables frequently with pancake turner, until crisp-tender, about 5 minutes. Do not overcook.

4 servings/30 calories each. (Each serving: about ½ cup.)

ITALIAN CABBAGE WEDGES

Cut 2-pound cabbage into 6 wedges; remove core. In large skillet, heat 1 inch salted water (½ teaspoon salt to 1 cup water) to boiling. Add cabbage; cover and heat to boiling. Cook until crisp-tender, 10 to 12 minutes; drain.

Place cabbage on serving platter. Cut three 1-ounce slices mozzarella cheese in half. Place half-slice cheese on each cabbage wedge. Garnish each with strip of pimiento and sprinkle with oregano leaves.

6 servings/75 calories each.

Make more of mealtime than just eating. Set a pretty table and generate lively conversation. Give everyone something to think about besides the food.

CELERY POLYNESIAN

1 teaspoon salad oil
5 cups ¼-inch diagonal slices
  celery
1 can (8½ ounces) water chestnuts,
  drained and sliced
1 tablespoon instant chicken
  bouillon
½ teaspoon salt
½ teaspoon celery salt
1 jar (2 ounces) sliced pimiento,
  drained

Heat oil in large skillet. Cook celery, water chestnuts, bouillon and seasonings in oil over medium heat, turning vegetables constantly with pancake turner, until celery is crisp-tender, about 10 minutes. Stir in pimiento and heat.

5 servings/45 calories each. (Each serving: 1 cup.)

Get back to nature. Learn to enjoy the built-in flavor of vegetables without butter, sauce or too much salt. Example: How long has it been since you washed and ate a tomato, right off the vine and seasoned with nothing but sunshine?

IRISH MASHED POTATOES

Cabbage makes potatoes go further with fewer calories—you'll be surprised how it perks up the texture, too!

---

2 cups shredded green cabbage
  (about ½ small)
Mashed potato puffs (enough
  for 4 servings)
¼ cup sliced green onion
Dash pepper

Heat ½ inch salted water (½ teaspoon salt to 1 cup water) to boiling. Add cabbage; cover and heat to boiling. Cook 5 minutes; drain.

Prepare mashed potato puffs as directed on package except—increase salt to ¾ teaspoon, omit butter and substitute skim milk for the milk. Fold in onion, pepper and hot cabbage.

6 servings/55 calories each. (Each serving: ⅔ cup.)

POTATO TOPPER AND DIP

¼ cup skim milk
2 cups 2% cottage cheese (small
  curd)
1 envelope (about 1½ ounces)
  onion soup mix

Place all ingredients in blender. Cover and blend on high speed until smooth and creamy. Cover and refrigerate at least 1 hour.

2 cups/15 calories per tablespoon.

MUSHROOM TOPPER

A flavorful accent for meat or fish. Pictured on page 38.

Cook and stir ½ pound mushrooms (if they are large, cut into slices), 1 teaspoon water and 1 teaspoon instant beef bouillon in skillet over medium heat until bouillon is dissolved and mushrooms are hot.

4 servings/20 calories each. (Each serving: ¼ cup.)

SEASONED MIXED VEGETABLES

Four different vegetables—some fresh, some frozen—all seasoned and cooked together in the same pan.

2 cups water
1 envelope (.77 ounce) bacon-flavored salad dressing mix
1 cup ¼-inch-thick carrot sticks
1 package (10 ounces) frozen cauliflower
1 package (6 ounces) frozen Chinese pea pods
1 cup mushrooms, trimmed
4 lettuce cups

Heat water and salad dressing mix in large saucepan to boiling, stirring occasionally. Add carrot sticks; heat to boiling. Cover and boil 2 minutes. Add frozen vegetables; heat to boiling. Cover and boil 2 minutes. Stir in mushrooms; remove from heat. Cool vegetables in liquid. Refrigerate about 3 hours. With slotted spoon, remove vegetables to lettuce cups.

4 servings/65 calories each. (Each serving: ¾ cup.)

EASY BROILED ZUCCHINI

Nice little slices of garlic-flavored squash. At 25 calories a serving, you can even afford to splurge with a sprinkle of grated cheese (30 calories a tablespoon). And it's so easy to stretch this recipe—simply add another squash or two.

Cut 4 small zucchini lengthwise in half. Set oven control at broil and/or 550°. Place slices cut sides up in broiler pan. Brush with salad oil and sprinkle with salt, garlic salt and pepper. Broil 3 inches from heat until tender, 6 to 10 minutes.

4 servings/25 calories each.

Get a new generation off on the right foot in eating. Reward with love, console with understanding, use food only to allay hunger.

SOUTHERN RICE AND TOMATOES WITH ARTICHOKES

1 can (14 ounces) artichoke
   hearts
1 can (16 ounces) stewed
   tomatoes
1½ cups uncooked instant rice
1 tablespoon dried shredded
   green onion or 3 green onions,
   cut up
¼ teaspoon salt

In large skillet, heat artichoke hearts (with liquid), tomatoes, rice, onion and salt to boiling, stirring frequently. Reduce heat; cover and simmer until rice is tender, about 10 minutes.

8 servings/100 calories each. (Each serving: ⅔ cup.)

SPINACH CONTINENTAL

2 packages (10 ounces each)
   frozen chopped spinach
1 can (4 ounces) mushroom stems
   and pieces, drained
   (reserve liquid)
1 can (8½ ounces) water
   chestnuts, drained and sliced
2 teaspoons instant minced
   onion
1½ teaspoons salt
¼ teaspoon garlic powder
1 carton (8 ounces) unflavored
   yogurt (1 cup)

Cook spinach as directed on package except—use reserved mushroom liquid and enough water (not salted) to measure ½ cup; drain. Stir in remaining ingredients. Heat over low heat, stirring occasionally, just until mixture simmers.

6 servings/80 calories each. (Each serving: ⅔ cup.)

DESSERTS— PURE PLEASURE AT LITTLE "PRICE"

Or
Any Day Can Have a Happy Ending

Fun. That's what desserts are. And lack of them can cause even the most dedicated calorie-counter to feel downhearted. Pangs of desire for a sweet may even scuttle the plans of the most earnest calorie-counter. To the rescue! The desserts in this chapter are the soul of sweet reasonableness— calorically speaking. Some are "extras," to eat after other nutritional needs have been met; others incorporate basic nutrients so artfully you'd never guess they were good for you. All, however, are calorie-cut to give you a treat without unbalancing your calorie budget.

FRESH PINEAPPLE TROPICALE

Pour ¼ cup orange-flavored liqueur on 3 cups cut-up fresh pineapple and toss. Divide among 6 dessert dishes and garnish each with a sprig of mint.

6 servings/75 calories each.

FRUIT-CHEESE BUFFET

If you like, use the jewel-colored fruits as a centerpiece, add cheese at dessert time. Pictured on page 55.

1 pound seedless green grapes, separated into small clusters
1 cantaloupe, pared and cut into thin wedges
⅛ watermelon (3 to 4 pounds), pared and cut into 2-inch pieces
1 pineapple, cut into rings, pared and cored
4 ounces mozzarella cheese, cut into 8 pieces
7-ounce Gouda cheese, cut into 14 wedges (casing left on)
½ pound dark sweet cherries
Lemon leaves

Mound grapes in center of large tray or serving plate. Arrange cantaloupe wedges and watermelon pieces alternately around grapes, then place pineapple rings and cheeses on plate. Garnish plate with cherries and lemon leaves.

About 10 servings/105 or 110 calories each. (Each serving: ½ cup fruit—65 calories; ½ ounce mozzarella cheese—40 calories, or 1 wedge (½ ounce) Gouda cheese—45 calories.)

PINK PEARS

4 pears, halved, pared and cored
1 can (12 ounces) low-calorie raspberry-flavored soda pop (no sugar), chilled
1 teaspoon cornstarch
1 tablespoon water
1 envelope (about 1½ ounces) whipped topping mix

Place pear halves cut sides down in large skillet. Add 1 cup of the soda pop; cover and simmer until pears are tender, 8 to 10 minutes. Place a pear half cut side up in each dessert dish.

Mix cornstarch and water; stir into liquid in skillet. Cook, stirring constantly, until mixture thickens and boils. Boil and stir 1 minute. Pour onto pear halves.

Prepare topping mix as directed on package except—substitute remaining soda pop (½ cup) for the milk. Spoon 1 tablespoon topping onto each serving.

8 servings/65 calories each.

SPARKLING FRUIT IN WINE

For two or twenty. The mandarin-orange version is pictured on page 56.

For each serving, place ¼ cup fresh fruit in goblet. Pour ⅓ cup wine over fruit. Serve immediately.

Combinations
Cantaloupe balls or mandarin orange segments and Chianti. (1 serving/75 calories.)

Strawberries or peach slices and rosé. (1 serving/75 calories.)

Pineapple tidbits or seedless green grapes and Rhine wine. (1 serving/75 calories with pineapple; 85 calories with grapes.)

WATERMELON CRYSTALS

Pretty as a picture. As a shortcut, liquefy melon in your blender.

2 cups sieved watermelon pulp
   (about 4 cups diced)
1 can (6 ounces) frozen lemonade
   concentrate, partially thawed
1 lemonade can water
2 egg whites
¼ cup sugar
3 or 4 drops red food color
6 watermelon balls
Mint leaves

Mix watermelon pulp, lemonade concentrate and water; pour into refrigerator tray. Freeze until mushy, 1½ to 2 hours (do not freeze until firm).

Beat egg whites in small mixer bowl until foamy. Beat in sugar, 1 tablespoon at a time; beat until stiff and glossy. Do not underbeat. Place watermelon mixture in chilled bowl; fold in meringue and food color. Turn into 2 refrigerator trays. Freeze, stirring once or twice, until firm. Serve in dessert dishes; garnish each serving with a watermelon ball and mint leaves.

6 servings/110 calories each.

Variations

Cantaloupe Crystals: Substitute 2 cups sieved cantaloupe pulp (about 1 medium) for the watermelon pulp and add 2 drops yellow food color. (6 servings/80 calories each.)

Honeydew Crystals: Substitute 2 cups sieved honeydew melon pulp for the watermelon pulp and green food color for the red food color. (6 servings/80 calories each.)

WATERMELON FRUIT BOWL

Spectacular showpiece for an outdoor buffet. A calorie-counter's bargain with or without wine.

Cut off lengthwise top third of large oblong watermelon, making a saw-toothed edge with sharp thin knife; cover and refrigerate top third for future use. Cut watermelon balls from larger section and refrigerate. Cut out remaining fruit, leaving a neat shell. Drain shell; cover and refrigerate.

At serving time, fill shell with watermelon balls, cantaloupe balls, pineapple chunks, banana slices, peach slices, strawberries, raspberries and blueberries or other fruits. Large shell will hold about 22 cups fruit. Drizzle 2 cans (6 ounces each) frozen pink lemonade concentrate (thawed) or 1½ cups dry sherry or rosé on fruit.

About 22 servings/70 to 85 calories each. (Each serving: 1 cup fruit—70 calories; with lemonade or rosé—80 calories, or with dry sherry—85 calories.)

Sweets without sugar. Cut calories (and lots of them!) with naturally sweet fruits—fresh, water-packed, canned in natural juices—and berries frozen unsweetened.

MIX AND MATCH YOUR OWN LOW-CALORIE DESSERT

Surprise! Dessert can be a calorie bargain. For instance, for 85 calories you can have ½ cup strawberries, 1 tablespoon Neufchâtel cheese spread and 2 triangle crackers.

Fruit	Calories	Fruit	Calories
1 plum (2-inch)	25	¼ honeydew melon (5-inch diameter)	35
½ cup grapes	35	1 medium peach	35
⅓ cup blueberries	30	1 medium apple	90
½ cup strawberries	30	1 medium orange	75
¼ cup dark sweet cherries	35	1 medium pear	100
¼ cantaloupe (5-inch diameter)	30		

Cheese Spreads	Calories	Crackers	Calories
1 tablespoon (½ ounce) pasteurized Neufchâtel cheese spread* with		1 pretzel stick	5
		1 pizza-flavored rye wafer	20
Onion	35	Melba toast round (garlic, rye, white)	10
Pimientos	35	Triangle cracker	10
Clams	35	Chicken-flavored cracker	10
Bacon and Horseradish	40	Ham-flavored cracker	10
Blue cheese	40	Barbecue-flavored cracker	15
Bacon	40	Shredded wheat wafer	20

*In 5-ounce jar.

COUNT THE CALORIES AHEAD OF TIME

Before you take your first bite, remember . . .

Calories in:	Equal Calories in:
1 chocolate éclair (315)	■ 5 cantaloupe halves
1 chocolate malt (500)	■ 14 fresh peaches
1 slice (1/16) 2-layer, 9-inch chocolate cake, frosted (235)	■ 4 cups fresh strawberries
½ cup salted peanuts (460)	■ 18 cups salted popcorn

ORANGE-COCONUT ANGEL

Prepare 1 package (15 or 16 ounces) white angel food cake mix as directed except—fold in 2 tablespoons grated orange peel and 2 tablespoons flaked coconut with the flour-sugar mixture. Invert .tube pan on funnel; let hang until cake is completely cool. Cut cake into 12 or 16 slices.

16 servings/115 calories each; 12 servings/155 calories each.

ORANGE FLUFF ANGEL

A wonderful dessert for a party or a holiday gathering of family and friends. Double the topping so non-dieters can indulge. The calorie-counters can use 2 tablespoons on their cake. Pictured on page 55.

2 eggs, beaten
¼ cup sugar
⅓ cup orange juice
1 tablespoon grated orange peel
1 envelope (about 1½ ounces)
  whipped topping mix
10-inch angel food cake

Cook eggs, sugar and orange juice over low heat, stirring constantly, until mixture thickens, about 10 minutes. Remove from heat; stir in orange peel and cool.

Prepare topping mix as directed on package except—substitute skim milk for the milk. Fold orange mixture into topping. Refrigerate 1 hour before serving; refrigerate any leftover topping.

Cut cake into 16 slices; top each slice with 2 tablespoons orange topping.

16 servings/145 calories each.

LAST-MINUTE ANGEL FOOD CAKE TOPPINGS

Evaporated Milk Topping
⅔ cup evaporated skim milk
¼ cup sugar
2 teaspoons lemon juice

Pour skim milk into small mixer bowl; place in freezer until ice crystals form around edge, about 30 minutes. Add sugar and lemon juice; beat until very thick and fluffy. Serve immediately. (Topping can also be refrigerated up to 1 hour or frozen for future use.)

2 cups/10 calories per tablespoon.

Egg White-Dry Milk Topping
½ cup nonfat dry milk
½ cup iced water
1 egg white
1 tablespoon lemon juice
¼ cup sugar
½ teaspoon vanilla

In small mixer bowl, beat dry milk, iced water and egg white on high speed 3 minutes. Add lemon juice; beat on high speed 1 minute. Beat in sugar, 1 tablespoon at a time; beat until very thick and fluffy. Blend in vanilla on low speed. Serve immediately or refrigerate no longer than 1 hour. Freeze any leftover topping and serve frozen.

4 cups/5 calories per tablespoon.

FROZEN LEMON GINGER PIE

An easy crumb crust is the base for this cool finale. Pictured on page 55.

1 teaspoon butter or margarine
⅓ cup fine gingersnap or vanilla wafer crumbs (about 6 cookies)
3 eggs, separated
½ cup sugar
1 cup frozen whipped topping (thawed)
1 tablespoon grated lemon peel
¼ cup lemon juice

Grease 9-inch pie pan with butter; sprinkle ¼ cup of the crumbs on bottom and side of pie pan. Beat egg whites until foamy. Beat in sugar, 1 tablespoon at a time; beat until stiff and glossy. Do not underbeat. Beat egg yolks until thick and lemon colored. Fold into meringue. Mix whipped topping, lemon peel and lemon juice; fold into egg mixture. Pour into pie pan; sprinkle remaining crumbs on top. Freeze until firm, 3 to 4 hours. Freeze any leftover pie.

8 servings/130 calories each.

When you get hungry (and you will), don't panic. Fill up on snacks (see some examples on page 35), or lose yourself in a "hungry job"—clean a drawer, weed the garden, give yourself a facial.

DANISH STRAWBERRY PIE WITH RICE CRUST

Prepare early in the day so the glaze will have time to set. The rice crust is a great calorie-saver. Pictured on page 55.

1 teaspoon butter or margarine
1 cup cooked regular rice
½ teaspoon vanilla
1 egg white
1 package (4¾ ounces) strawberry-flavored pudding and pie filling
1½ teaspoons grated lemon peel
1 quart strawberries
½ cup frozen whipped topping (thawed)

Heat oven to 350°. Grease 9-inch pie pan with butter. Beat rice, vanilla and egg white with fork. Turn mixture into pie pan; spread evenly with rubber scraper on bottom and halfway up side of pie pan. (Do not leave any holes.) Bake 5 minutes. Cool.

Prepare pudding and pie filling as directed on package for pie filling. Stir in lemon peel; cool.

If strawberries are large, cut into halves. Arrange in pie shell. Carefully pour strawberry filling over strawberries. Refrigerate at least 6 hours. Run knife around edge to loosen crust. Cut into wedges and top each wedge with 1 tablespoon whipped topping.

8 servings/130 calories each.

CUSTARD PIE WITH RICE CRUST

Skim milk in the custard, rice as a crust and you've trimmed 100 calories or more a serving from the traditional custard pie.

1 teaspoon butter or margarine
1 cup cooked regular rice
¼ teaspoon cinnamon
1 egg white
2 eggs plus 1 egg yolk
½ cup sugar
¼ teaspoon salt
2 cups skim milk, scalded
½ teaspoon vanilla
Nutmeg

Heat oven to 350°. Grease 9-inch pie pan with butter. Beat rice, cinnamon and egg white with fork. Turn mixture into pie pan; spread evenly with rubber scraper on bottom and halfway up side of pie pan. (Do not leave any holes.) Bake 5 minutes.

Beat eggs, egg yolk, sugar, salt, skim milk and vanilla thoroughly. Carefully pour into hot rice crust. Sprinkle with nutmeg. Bake until knife inserted 1 inch from edge comes out clean, about 25 minutes. Immediately run knife around edge to loosen crust. Refrigerate.

8 servings/135 calories each.

Substitutions
For the cinnamon: ¼ teaspoon nutmeg, mace, almond extract or vanilla.

INDIVIDUAL APRICOT CHEESECAKES

Lower-calorie Neufchâtel cheese and an absence of crust put these rich treats within the calorie-counter's reach.

2 eggs, separated
½ cup sugar
1½ packages (8-ounce size) Neufchâtel cheese, softened
1 teaspoon vanilla
8 dried apricots, finely chopped
2 tablespoons apricot preserves

Heat oven to 350°. Line 12 medium muffin cups with paper baking cups. Beat egg whites in small mixer bowl until foamy. Beat in sugar, 1 tablespoon at a time; beat until stiff and glossy. Do not underbeat.

In large mixer bowl, blend cheese, egg yolks and vanilla on low speed, scraping bowl constantly, 1 minute. Beat on high speed, scraping bowl occasionally, until mixture is smooth and fluffy, about 2 minutes. Stir in apricots. Fold meringue into cheese mixture. Divide among muffin cups. Bake until knife inserted in center of one comes out clean, about 20 minutes. Refrigerate until serving time.

Remove paper cups and top each serving with ½ teaspoon apricot preserves.

12 servings/145 calories each.

NOTE: Cheesecakes can be frozen up to 2 weeks. Remove to refrigerator about 20 minutes before serving.

ROSY PEACHES FLAMBE

Evaporated Milk Whip (below)
  or Dry Milk Whip (page 60)
¼ cup currant jelly
½ cup low-calorie strawberry-
  flavored soda pop (no sugar)
4 large peaches, peeled and sliced
1 teaspoon lemon juice
¼ cup brandy

Prepare whip as directed except—turn whip into refrigerator tray and freeze at least 8 hours.

Heat jelly and soda pop in saucepan or chafing dish, stirring constantly, until jelly is melted and mixture is smooth. Stir in peach slices; cook over low heat until peaches are almost tender, about 3 minutes. Stir in lemon juice.

Cut frozen whip into 6 servings and place in dessert dishes. Heat brandy in long-handled ladle or small saucepan but do not boil. Ignite and pour over hot peach mixture. Stir sauce and peaches and spoon onto frozen whip.

6 servings/75 calories each.

Evaporated Milk Whip

⅓ cup evaporated skim milk
1 teaspoon unflavored gelatin
1 tablespoon water
2 tablespoons sugar
½ teaspoon vanilla

Pour milk into small mixer bowl; place in freezer until crystals form around edge, about 30 minutes.

Sprinkle gelatin on water to soften. Place over boiling water until gelatin is dissolved. Add sugar and vanilla to milk; beat on high speed until very thick and fluffy. Gradually beat in gelatin until mixture is very stiff. Serve immediately. (Or whip can be refrigerated up to 1 hour or frozen for making Root Beer in the Clouds [page 60] or Rosy Peaches Flambé [left].)

2 cups/5 calories per tablespoon.

ROCKY ROAD CHEESE-FRUIT WHIP

To vary the color and flavor use cherry-, strawberry- or orange-flavored gelatin. Pictured on page 17.

1 envelope low-calorie
  lime-flavored gelatin
¾ cup 2% cottage cheese
1 carton (4½ ounces) frozen
  whipped topping (thawed)
1 drop green food color (optional)
1 cup honeydew melon balls
1 can (8 ounces) crushed
  pineapple in unsweetened
  pineapple juice, drained
2 tablespoons snipped mint leaves

Sprinkle gelatin on cottage cheese to soften. Stir in and let stand a few minutes. Stir again until gelatin is dissolved. Fold in whipped topping, food color and fruits. Cover and refrigerate until serving time. Divide among 6 dessert dishes and garnish with mint leaves.

6 servings/125 calories each.

RASPBERRY DE-LUSCIOUS

As good as its name implies, this frozen dessert goes together literally in minutes and adds only 105 calories per serving. Pictured on page 56.

1 package (10 ounces) frozen raspberries, thawed and drained (reserve syrup)
1 tablespoon lemon juice
½ cup sugar
1 egg white
1 carton (4½ ounces) frozen whipped topping (thawed)

Place raspberries in small mixer bowl. Measure reserved raspberry syrup; set aside ½ cup and pour remaining syrup into bowl. Add remaining ingredients except whipped topping; beat on low speed 1 minute. Beat on high speed, scraping bowl occasionally, until mixture is thick and fluffy, about 3 minutes. Fold in 1 cup of the whipped topping. Spread in ungreased baking pan, 8 x 8 x 2 inches. Freeze until firm, about 2 hours.

Just before serving, fold reserved ½ cup raspberry syrup into remaining whipped topping. Cut frozen dessert into squares and top each with about 2 tablespoons topping.

9 servings/105 calories each.

Variation

Peach De-luscious: Substitute 1 package (10 ounces) frozen peach slices for the frozen raspberries; sprinkle nutmeg over each serving. (9 servings/105 calories each.)

FAST FROZEN FRUIT

Thaw orange juice concentrate just enough to beat—the colder it is, the faster the milk will "whip." Pictured on page 56.

1 envelope unflavored gelatin
3 tablespoons water
1 can (6 ounces) frozen orange juice concentrate, partially thawed
1 cup nonfat dry milk
1 tablespoon sugar
1 banana, sliced
1 can (8 ounces) crushed pineapple in unsweetened pineapple juice, drained
1 can (16 ounces) fruit cocktail in water pack, drained
Mint leaves

Sprinkle gelatin on water to soften. Heat over medium heat, stirring constantly, until gelatin is dissolved, about 3 minutes.

In small mixer bowl, beat orange juice concentrate and dry milk on low speed 1 minute, scraping bowl occasionally. Beat on high speed until smooth and fluffy. Gradually beat in gelatin and sugar; beat until very thick.

Fold in banana, pineapple and fruit cocktail. Pour into baking pan, 8 x 8 x 2 inches. Freeze until firm, about 2 hours. Remove to refrigerator ½ hour before serving. Cut into 9 servings. Garnish with mint leaves.

9 servings/125 calories each.

CHOCOLATE-MINT SNOWCAPS

A lighter-than-light fluffy pudding dessert. Pictured on page 56.

1 envelope (about 1½ ounces) whipped topping mix
¼ teaspoon peppermint extract
1 drop green or red food color
1 can (17.5 ounces) chocolate fudge pudding

Prepare topping mix as directed on package except—substitute skim milk for the milk and peppermint extract for the vanilla. Remove ½ cup of the topping to small bowl; fold in food color. Fold pudding into remaining topping.

Divide pudding mixture among 8 dessert dishes; top each with 1 tablespoon colored topping. Freeze no longer than 2 hours. Remove from freezer 15 minutes before serving.

8 servings/120 calories each. (Each serving: ½ cup.)

COCOA MALLOW

8 large marshmallows
¾ cup skim milk
2 tablespoons cocoa
½ teaspoon vanilla
Dash salt
1 envelope (about 1½ ounces) whipped topping mix

Heat marshmallows, skim milk and cocoa in small saucepan over medium heat, stirring constantly, until marshmallows are melted. Stir in vanilla and salt. Let stand at room temperature about 30 minutes.

Prepare topping mix as directed on package except—substitute skim milk for the milk. Reserve 2 tablespoons of the topping; fold cocoa mixture into remaining topping just until mixture is marbled. Divide among 6 dessert dishes. Top each with 1 teaspoon reserved topping. Refrigerate about 1 hour.

6 servings/125 calories each.

POTS DE CREME

Chocolate-flecked puddings—each serving is minus nearly 100 calories from its traditional counterpart.

¾ cup evaporated skim milk
⅓ cup sugar
¼ cup cocoa
1 teaspoon unflavored gelatin
⅛ teaspoon salt
1 egg, beaten
⅓ cup evaporated skim milk
1 teaspoon vanilla
Frozen whipped topping (thawed)

Pour ¾ cup skim milk into small mixer bowl; place in freezer until ice crystals form around edge, about 30 minutes.

Mix sugar, cocoa, gelatin, salt, egg and ⅓ cup skim milk in small saucepan until smooth. Cook over low heat, stirring constantly, until slightly thickened, about 5 minutes. Remove from heat; stir in vanilla and set aside.

Beat chilled milk on high speed until very thick and fluffy. Carefully fold in cocoa mixture, 1 tablespoon at a time. Divide among 8 demitasse cups or small dessert dishes. Refrigerate no longer than 1 hour. Top each serving with 1 teaspoon whipped topping.

8 servings/85 calories each.

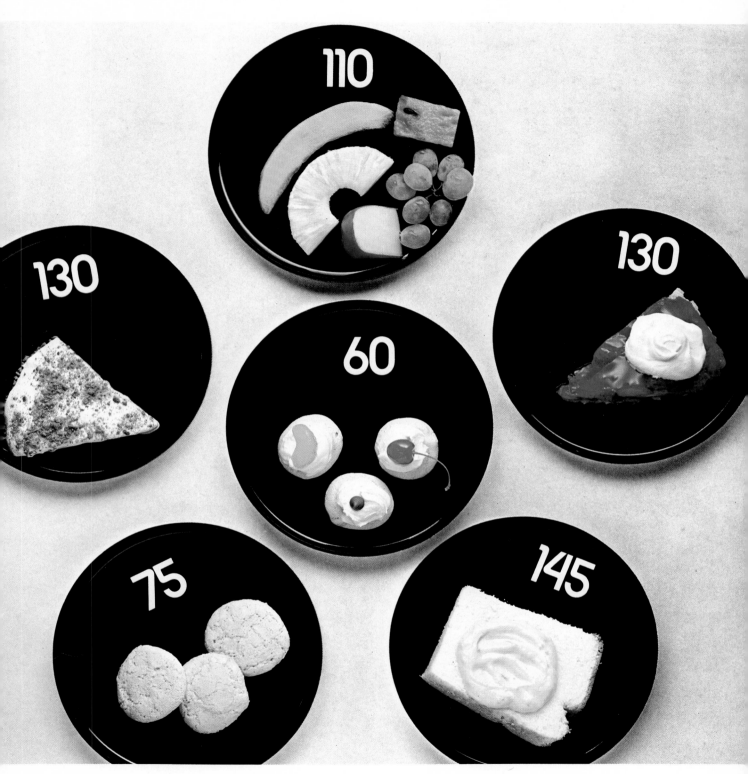

110—Fruit-Cheese Buffet (page 46); **130**—Frozen Lemon Ginger Pie (page 50); **75**—Tinted Angel Macaroons (page 59); **145**—Orange Fluff Angel (page 49); **130**—Danish Strawberry Pie with Rice Crust (page 50); **60**—Cocoa Mini-Meringues (page 58).

125—Fast Frozen Fruit (page 53); 120—Chocolate-Mint Snowcaps (page 54); 105—Raspberry De-luscious (page 53); 90—Frozen Almond Meringue (page 58); 75—Sparkling Fruit in Wine (page 46).

HOMEMADE LIME SHERBET

A real refresher. Pictured on page 36.

¾ cup boiling water
1 envelope low-calorie
  lime-flavored gelatin
½ cup sugar
1½ cups buttermilk
1½ teaspoons grated lemon peel
3 tablespoons lemon juice

Pour boiling water on gelatin and sugar in small mixer bowl; stir until gelatin and sugar are dissolved. Stir in remaining ingredients. Place in freezer until thickened but not set.

Beat until fluffy; pour into refrigerator tray and freeze until firm.

8 servings/70 calories each. (Each serving: ½ cup.)

SPOON-UP EGGNOGS

A Southern-style dessert. Pictured on page 37.

2 eggs, separated
Dash salt
¼ cup light rum or 1 tablespoon
  rum flavoring
1 carton (4½ ounces) frozen
  whipped topping (thawed)
Nutmeg

Beat egg whites until stiff. Beat egg yolks and salt in small mixer bowl until thick and lemon colored, about 5 minutes. Stir in rum. Fold whipped topping into egg yolks, then fold in whites. Divide among 6 cups; sprinkle wtih nutmeg and freeze. Serve frozen.

6 servings/75 calories each with rum flavoring; 95 calories each with rum. (Each serving: ½ cup.)

MAPLE FRANGO

A frozen delight that tastes like rich, pure cream but (of course) isn't. Use leftover egg whites for Frozen Almond Meringue (page 58).

½ cup evaporated skim milk
4 egg yolks
½ cup maple-flavored syrup
½ teaspoon vanilla
Chocolate Curls (below) or
  dash instant coffee

Pour skim milk into bowl; place in freezer until ice crystals form around edge, about 30 minutes.

While milk chills, beat egg yolks in small mixer bowl until thick and lemon colored. Heat syrup just to boiling. Pour about half the hot syrup very slowly in a thin stream into egg yolks, beating constantly on medium speed. Stir egg yolk mixture into syrup in pan. Cook over low heat, stirring constantly, until slightly thickened. Cool.

Beat milk and vanilla until very thick and fluffy. Fold in egg yolk mixture. Pour into refrigerator tray. Freeze until firm, at least 4 hours. Cut into 6 servings and garnish each with a Chocolate Curl.

6 servings/125 calories each.

Chocolate Curls
With vegetable parer or sharp thin knife, cut across block of semisweet or unsweetened chocolate with long thin strokes.

FROZEN ALMOND MERINGUE

Snowy base for your favorite fruit. Pictured on page 56. For greater volume, bring egg whites to room temperature before you beat them; refrigerate leftover yolks (no longer than a few days) to make Maple Frango (page 57).

4 egg whites
¼ cup sugar
1 envelope (about 1½ ounces) whipped topping mix
1 teaspoon almond extract
4½ cups fresh fruit (strawberries, peaches, blueberries and/or raspberries)

Beat egg whites in large mixer bowl until foamy. Beat in sugar, 1 tablespoon at a time; beat until stiff but not dry. Prepare topping mix as directed on package except—substitute skim milk for the milk. Fold topping and almond extract into egg whites. Turn into ungreased baking pan, 8 x 8 x 2 inches. Freeze until firm, at least 4 hours. Cut into 9 squares; top each square with ½ cup fruit.

9 servings/90 calories each.

Bargain bonus. A tablespoon of commercial whipped topping costs a mere 10-15 calories or even less. Check labels for accurate counts.

COCOA MINI-MERINGUES

Three of these little confections total only 60 calories. Pictured on page 55.

3 egg whites
¼ teaspoon cream of tartar
¾ cup sugar
2 tablespoons cocoa
Frozen whipped topping (thawed)
Fresh fruit, semisweet chocolate pieces or maraschino cherries

Heat oven to 275°. Cover 2 baking sheets with aluminum foil. Beat egg whites and cream of tartar in small mixer bowl until foamy. Beat in sugar, 1 tablespoon at a time; beat until stiff and glossy. Do not underbeat. Sprinkle cocoa on meringue and gently fold in.

Drop meringue by level measuring-tablespoonfuls about 1½ inches apart onto baking sheets. Make small indentation in center of each with tip of teaspoon. Bake 10 minutes. Turn off oven; leave meringues in oven with door closed 1 hour. Remove from oven; finish cooling meringues away from draft.

Top each meringue with 1 teaspoon whipped topping and 1 piece fresh fruit. Wrap leftover plain or topped meringues in aluminum foil; freeze up to 2 weeks.

48 meringues/20 calories each.

Variation
Three-in-One Meringues: Omit cocoa; divide meringue into 3 parts (about 1 cup each). Fold into each part one of the following:
¼ teaspoon powdered instant coffee
2 teaspoons cocoa
½ teaspoon grated orange or lemon peel
¼ teaspoon almond or peppermint extract

TINTED ANGEL MACAROONS

If you want to save time by making these larger, drop them by ordinary teaspoonfuls; you'll get 6 dozen, at 35 calories each. Pictured on page 55.

1 package (16 ounces) one-step white angel food cake mix
½ cup low-calorie strawberry- or orange-flavored soda pop (no sugar)
1½ teaspoons almond extract
1 package (7 ounces) cookie coconut (about 2 cups)

Heat oven to 350°. Cover baking sheet with aluminum foil or heavy brown paper. In large mixer bowl, blend cake mix, soda pop and almond extract on low speed, scraping bowl constantly, ½ minute. Beat on medium speed, scraping bowl occasionally, 1 minute. Fold in coconut. Drop batter by measuring-teaspoonfuls about 2 inches apart onto baking sheet. Bake until set, 10 to 12 minutes. Slide foil, with cookies, onto wire rack; cool cookies completely before removing from foil. Store cookies in freezer or between layers of waxed paper in a box.

About 8 dozen cookies/25 calories each.

Variation
Fruit Macaroons: Substitute water for the soda pop, vanilla for the almond extract and 1 cup chopped dried apricots, figs or prunes for the coconut. (About 8 dozen cookies/25 calories each.)

SOUR LEMON COOKIES

Heat oven to 375°. Prepare 1 package (18.5 ounces) yellow cake mix as directed except—decrease water to ½ cup and use 2 eggs; omit salad oil. Beat just until ingredients are mixed. Drop batter by measuring-teaspoonfuls 2 inches apart onto greased baking sheet. Bake until light brown on edges, 6 to 8 minutes. Immediately remove from baking sheet and cool on wire rack. Spread ½ teaspoon Lemon Glaze (below) on each cookie.

About 8 dozen cookies/40 calories each.

Lemon Glaze
Mix 2 cups confectioners' sugar, 2 tablespoons grated lemon peel and ¼ cup lemon juice until smooth.

Variation
Chocolate Cookies: Substitute 1 package (18.5 ounces) devils food cake mix for the yellow cake mix. Omit glaze and drop a dab (¼ teaspoon) of canned dark Dutch fudge frosting on top of each cookie. (About 8 dozen cookies/30 calories each.)

Mix iced tea and low-calorie ginger ale for a sparkly summer cooler. A refreshing thirst-quencher for everyone.

FOAMING SODA POP

For each serving, fill tall glass ⅓ full with chilled low-calorie favorite-flavored soda pop (no sugar). Stir in 2 tablespoons nonfat dry milk (it will foam up and fill the glass). Serve immediately. Pour in additional soda pop as needed.

1 serving/30 calories.

Half the fun is in the fizz—so be sure the low-calorie soda pop you use for these recipes is carbonated!

ROOT BEER IN THE CLOUDS

A drink that doubles as dessert. Pictured on page 38.

For each serving, place ⅓ cup Dry Milk Whip (below) or Evaporated Milk Whip (page 52) in tall glass. Pour ½ can (12-ounce size) chilled low-calorie root beer (no sugar) into glass. Serve immediately.

1 serving/30 calories.

Dry Milk Whip
½ teaspoon unflavored gelatin
2 tablespoons sugar
3 tablespoons nonfat dry milk
½ cup water
½ teaspoon vanilla

Mix gelatin, sugar and dry milk in small saucepan. Stir in water. Heat over medium heat, stirring until gelatin is dissolved, about 3 minutes. Stir in vanilla. Pour into small mixer bowl. Refrigerate until slightly thickened.

Beat on high speed until stiff peaks form. Serve immediately. (Or topping can be refrigerated up to 1 hour or frozen for making Root Beer in the Clouds [above] or Rosy Peaches Flambé [page 52].) (2 cups/5 calories per tablespoon.)

A CRAM COURSE IN CALORIE-CUTTING

Or
What You Can Eat and When

No two ways about it, cutting calories takes a bit of doing. It's rather like enrolling in a college course. Just signing up isn't enough—you still have to do the homework and show up for classes. In this chapter we give you an outline of the curriculum—guidelines for breakfast (very significant), required reading for lunch at home or on the job, a few formulas for party plans. And for those inevitable moments of yawning emptiness, there's a list of sturdy stopgaps with calories counted—all calculated to earn you an A in your slimming course.

I can save both time and calories in the morning by going without breakfast. Is that a good idea?

It's one of the worst. Breakfast is definitely not for skipping. The time you think you will save by not sitting down to a good start-the-day meal will inevitably be lost later in the morning, when you bog down from a lack of energy. Whatever pleases the taste—*and provides at least one-fourth of your nutritional needs for the day* (see page 6)—can be breakfast. (One serving from each of the basic four food groups is a good, easy-to-remember guide.) Besides, you'll have the rest of the day to "work it off." Following are some good choices:

BREAKFAST IS A CALORIE-COUNTER'S MOST IMPORTANT MEAL

Fruits, Beverages	Calories	Fruits, Beverages	Calories
1 medium grapefruit half	50	4 ounces unsweetened pineapple juice	70
1 medium orange	75	4 ounces tomato juice	25
1 cantaloupe half (5-inch diameter)	60	8 ounces skim milk	90
4 ounces orange juice	55	Coffee or tea	0
4 ounces apricot nectar	70		

Meats, Cereals, Breads	Calories	Meats, Cereals, Breads	Calories
1 cup corn flake cereal	100	1 slice Canadian-style bacon	65
1 cup presweetened corn flake cereal	155	1 egg, boiled or poached	80
		1 slice toast	65
1 cup whole wheat flake cereal	105	1 slice French toast	185
½ cup oatmeal	65	1 four-inch pancake	60

Extras	Calories	Extras	Calories
1 teaspoon sugar	15	1 tablespoon low-calorie syrup	2
1 teaspoon butter or margarine	35	1 tablespoon Low-Calorie Grape Jelly (page 63)	5

NOTE: Avoid bacon, fried eggs (except those fried in skillet coated with vegetable spray-on for cookware), coffee cakes, doughnuts and jelly or jam—they're all high in calories! Reduce calories in French toast and pancakes (see chart) by using skim milk and coating the griddle with vegetable spray-on for cookware.

I carry my lunch. Can I save calories?

Count calories before they go into the bag. Add color, sparkle and crunch with fresh fruit . . . crisp vegetable snacks . . . kabob of cooked meat, cheese and fruit or vegetable . . . cottage cheese or cold salad makings with low-calorie dressing in leakproof pill bottle. Here are some more tote-able ideas:

OPEN-FACE CHICKEN SANDWICH

A good idea for lunching or healthy snacking. Pictured on page 38.

Spread 1½ teaspoons low-calorie Thousand Island dressing on Lacy Melba Toast (right) or on thin slice French or Vienna bread. Top with slices of smoked chicken (1 ounce). Garnish with 1 teaspoon currant jelly and several Pickled Cucumber slices (page 34).

1 sandwich/110 calories.

LOW-CALORIE GRAPE JELLY

1 cup unsweetened grape juice
1 cup low-calorie grape-flavored soda pop (no sugar)
1 envelope unflavored gelatin
1 or 2 drops red food color (optional)

Measure grape juice and soda pop into small saucepan. Sprinkle gelatin on liquid to soften. Stir over medium heat until gelatin is dissolved, about 3 minutes. Heat to boiling. Stir in food color. Immediately pour into two 1-cup jelly glasses. Cool. Cover and refrigerate until thickened. Store in refrigerator; keep no longer than 3 weeks.

2 glasses/5 calories per tablespoon.

LACY MELBA TOAST

Use as a base for an open-face sandwich or as a crunchy "go-with" for many a main dish. Pictured on page 38.

Place unsliced 1-pound loaf Vienna white bread or rye bread in freezer 1 hour. Cut with electric knife into thin slices (⅛ to ¼ inch). If desired, cut each slice into halves or thirds.

Heat oven to 325°. Arrange slices in single layer on ungreased baking sheet. If desired, sprinkle some slices with garlic salt, onion salt or ¼ teaspoon cinnamon-sugar (mixture of 1 tablespoon sugar and ½ teaspoon cinnamon). Bake until crisp and golden brown around edges, 12 to 15 minutes. Toast can be packed in box and used as needed.

60 slices/20 calories each; 25 calories each with cinnamon-sugar.

CRUNCHY COTTAGE CHEESE

A colorful and zesty accompaniment. Pictured on page 38.

1 carton (12 ounces) 2% cottage cheese (1½ cups)
½ green pepper, finely chopped, or ½ cup chopped celery
1 dill pickle, finely chopped
1 tablespoon freeze-dried chives
Salt

Mix cottage cheese, green pepper, dill pickle and chives; season with salt. Nice to spread on slices of unbuttered dark bread (60 calories each) or on small melba toast rounds (8 calories each).

1¾ cups/15 calories per tablespoon. (Makes enough for 6 to 8 slices bread.)

I'm at home for lunch—everything tempts me. What's a good way to hold calories down?

See page 39 for a lunch under the 300-mark. Or fill up on an open-face sandwich (page 63) or on one of these super soups:

GERMAN-STYLE VEGETABLE SOUP

3 cups reserved pork broth*
1 can (8 ounces) sauerkraut
1 bay leaf
½ to 1 teaspoon salt
1 cup thinly sliced carrot
1 cup diagonal slices celery
2 medium tomatoes, peeled and cut into wedges
¼ cup barley
2 tablespoons snipped parsley

Skim fat from broth. Cut through sauerkraut (while it's still in the can) with kitchen scissors. Heat broth, sauerkraut (with liquid) and remaining ingredients except parsley to boiling. Reduce heat; cover and cook until carrot is tender, 25 to 30 minutes. Remove bay leaf. Serve in soup bowls and sprinkle with parsley.

6 servings/70 calories each. (Each serving: 1 cup.)

*Reserved broth from Pork Roll (page 15); if necessary, add water to measure 3 cups. Canned chicken broth or beef broth (bouillon) can be substituted for the pork broth.

HEARTY VEGETABLE SOUP

2 cans (12 ounces each) vegetable juice cocktail
2 cups water
1 small cabbage (about 1 pound), finely chopped
1 medium onion, sliced
3 small or 2 medium carrots, sliced
½ cup chopped celery
2 tablespoons instant beef or chicken bouillon

Heat all ingredients to boiling. Reduce heat; cover and simmer 1 hour.

8 servings/45 calories each. (Each serving: 1 cup.)

NOTE: Cabbage can be chopped in blender. Cut cabbage into 2-inch pieces. Place half the pieces in blender; cover with water and chop, watching carefully. Drain thoroughly. Repeat with remaining cabbage.

ROSY CONSOMME

3½ cups water
1 tablespoon plus 1 teaspoon instant beef bouillon or 4 cubes beef bouillon
1 cup tomato juice
6 unpared cucumber slices

Heat all ingredients except cucumber slices to boiling, stirring occasionally. Serve hot in cups—or let consommé cool; serve in cups over ice. Garnish each with a cucumber slice.

6 servings/10 calories each. (Each serving: ¾ cup.)

QUICK SPINACH SOUP

A delicious 5-minute soup. Pictured on page 38.

2½ cups water
 1 tablespoon instant beef or
   chicken bouillon
 1 package (10 ounces) frozen
   chopped spinach
 1 can (4 ounces) mushroom stems
   and pieces
 1 jar (2 ounces) sliced pimiento,
   drained
 ½ teaspoon garlic salt
Dash rosemary leaves
Thin unpared cucumber slices or
   5 tablespoons unflavored yogurt

Heat water, bouillon and spinach to boiling; break spinach apart with fork. Cover and cook until tender, about 3 minutes. Stir in mushrooms (with liquid), pimiento, garlic salt and rosemary leaves; heat. Divide among 5 soup bowls and garnish each with cucumber slices or yogurt.

5 servings/30 calories each. (Each serving: 1 cup.)

I buy my lunch. How can I count calories?

Go to a cafeteria when possible—eyes forward past the desserts. Choose meats without gravy . . . salads with lemon juice instead of dressing . . . clear or vegetable soups. If hamburger is your choice, ask for it on unbuttered toast (65 calories versus 120 for a bun). Avoid lunch counter desserts; bring an orange or apple to eat at coffee time instead. Carry vegetable snacks to fill up on before or after lunch.

How can I count calories at a friend's dinner party without losing the friend?

Save your calories before the big dinner. Offer to bring some food for the dinner, then furnish a low-calorie addition to the menu (maybe a low-calorie fruit and melon boat like the one below). Serve yourself smaller portions of rich foods, giant helpings of salads and vegetables. Ask for a smaller dessert, then leave some on your plate. Suggest an after-dinner walk or game of table tennis. Get out the jump rope after you get home. Cut down on calories the next day.

FRUIT KABOBS IN WATERMELON BOAT

 1 round watermelon
 1 medium cantaloupe
 1 can (15¼ ounces) pineapple
   chunks in unsweetened
   pineapple juice, drained
 ¾ pound dark sweet cherries
 1 pint strawberries

Cut watermelon horizontally in half, making a saw-toothed edge with sharp thin knife; cut melon balls from top half. Cut thin slice from bottom half so watermelon will stand upright. Remove fruit from bottom half to just below saw-toothed edge.

Cut balls from cantaloupe. On each of about 40 bamboo skewers, place watermelon ball, cantaloupe ball, pineapple chunk, cherry and strawberry. Insert kabobs upright in watermelon boat.

About 20 servings/100 calories each. (Each serving: 2 kabobs.)

How can I avoid alcoholic drinks without calling attention to my weight problem?

Try some fake-out drinks. Drink iced coffee, tea or water in a fancy glass with an orange slice or bruised mint. Away from home, ask for club soda (no calories) with a twist of lime, a bloody Mary without the vodka (cutting calories to 60 for 6 ounces) or a screwdriver without vodka (about 90 calories for the orange juice alone).

But sometimes I really feel like a drink! Can I fit one into my eating plan?

Yes, but strictly as an extra! Two 3½-ounce Manhattans cost 230 calories; two martinis, 280; two beers, 230. A 1½-ounce jigger of liquor adds about 100 calories to any mixed drink, to say nothing of salted peanuts (460 calories for ½ cup) and other high-calorie snacks that accompany a drink.

Instead, try your favorite drink stretched with low-calorie soda. Or drink whiskey with water or soda with lots of ice for a long drink.

Or something new—one of these wine drinks:

WINE SNOWBALL

Freeze ⅔ cup dry red wine and 1⅓ cups low-calorie ginger ale (no sugar) or club soda in refrigerator tray until mushy, about 2 hours. Spoon into 2 sherbet dishes; garnish each with a strawberry.

2 servings/65 calories each. (Each serving: 1 cup.)

WINE WITH FRUIT KABOB

For each serving, pour ⅓ cup dry red wine and ⅔ cup low-calorie ginger ale (no sugar) into tall glass. Add ice cubes or crushed ice to fill glass. Place 2 seedless green grapes, 1 pineapple chunk and 1 strawberry on bamboo skewer; place in glass.

1 serving/70 calories.

WINE COOLER WITH CHEESE AND CRACKERS

For each serving, pour ¼ cup chilled dry red wine and ½ cup chilled club soda into goblet. Serve with 1 soda cracker, 2 melba toast rounds, ⅓ ounce Camembert cheese and ⅓ ounce pasteurized Neufchâtel cheese spread.

1 serving/125 calories.

I'm having guests for dinner. They aren't counting calories! What shall I do?

Ah—now's your challenge and your opportunity! Plan a low-calorie dinner so colorful and good tasting no one will think about calories. Then figure out your allowed calories, watch your own portions, and enjoy!

SAMPLE MENUS

TEENAGE KITCHEN PARTY
8 servings/375 calories each

Cantaloupe Wedges
(¼ melon each serving,
5 inches in diameter)
Chili with Yellow Beans
(double recipe, page 12)
Mexican Salad
(page 32)
Cloverleaf Rolls
(1 roll, 1 teaspoon
butter each serving)
Root Beer in the Clouds
(page 60)

COZY FIRESIDE DINNER
6 servings/420 calories each

Antipasto Tray:
Garlic Pickles,
Vegetable Snacks (page 35),
Pickled Artichokes (page 34)
Chicken with Mushroom Gravy
(page 20)
Spinach Salad
(1 cup each serving)
with Lemon Wedges
Baked Potatoes
(1 small potato, 1 tablespoon
Potato Topper
each serving, page 42)
Rosy Peaches Flambé
(page 52)

CALORIE-COUNTER'S LUNCHEON
8 servings/400 calories each

Dilled Fish Sticks
(triple recipe, page 24)
Gazpacho Mold
(page 33)
Spinach Continental
(double recipe, page 44)
Rye Wafers
(3 wafers each serving)
Fruit-Cheese Buffet
(page 46)

CELEBRATION SUPPER
8 servings/380 calories each

Party Round Steak
(page 10)
Crisp Vegetable Snacks
(page 35)
Poppy Seed Noodles
(½ cup each serving, page 19)
Asparagus Cuts
(½ cup each serving)
Melba Toast Rounds
(2 rounds each serving)
Pots de Crème
(page 54)

CALORIE CHART

Apple (1 med.)	90
Apple juice (½ cup)	60
Applesauce, canned (½ cup)	
sweetened	115
unsweetened	50
Apricots, canned (½ cup)	
sweetened	110
unsweetened	40
Apricots, fresh (3 med.)	55
Asparagus (½ cup)	20
Bacon (2 med. slices)	90
Bacon-flavored vegetable	
protein chips (4 tbsp.)	115
Banana (6″)	80
Beans (½ cup)	
green	15
navy	110
Beef, lean, trimmed (3 oz.)	
chuck	180
corned	185
dried or chipped	175
ground, lean (11% fat)	185
ground, regular (20% fat)	245
liver, fried	195
roast, rump	180
steak, flank	170
steak, Porterhouse,	
T-bone	190
steak, round	165
steak, sirloin	175
Beer (8 oz.)	115
Beets (½ cup)	25
Beverage, carbonated (8 oz.)	
cola-type, sweetened	95
fruit-flavored	115
ginger ale	75
low-calorie (refer to label)	
root beer	100
tonic water	80
Biscuit (2″ diam.)	100
Blueberries, fresh (⅓ cup)	30
Bologna (3 x ⅛″ slice)	80
Bread (1 slice)	
French, raisin or rye	60
white or whole wheat	65
Broccoli (½ cup)	20
Brussels sprouts (½ cup)	30
Butter, regular (1 tbsp.)	100
Butter, whipped (1 tbsp.)	65
Buttermilk, skim (8 oz.)	90

Cabbage, raw (½ cup)	10
Cake	
angel (1/12 of 10″ diam.)	135
chocolate (2-layer,	
chocolate icing,	
1/16 of 9″ diam.)	235
fruit (1/30 of 8″ loaf)	55
pound (½″ slice)	140
sponge (1/12 of 10″ diam.)	195
yellow (2-layer,	
chocolate icing,	
1/16 of 9″ diam.)	275
Cantaloupe (½ of 5″ diam.)	60
Caramel (1 med.)	40
Carrots, raw or cooked	
(½ cup or one 5″ long)	25
Catsup (1 tbsp.)	15
Cauliflower (½ cup)	15
Celery, raw (8″ stalk)	5
Cereal, cooked (½ cup)	
farina	50
oatmeal	65
Cereal, dry (1 cup)	
bran flakes	105
corn, puffed	100
corn, puffed,	
presweetened	115
corn flakes	100
corn flakes, presweetened	155
oats, puffed	100
wheat flakes	105
wheat germ (3 tbsp.)	100
Cheese	
American (1 oz.)	105
blue or Roquefort (1 oz.)	105
Camembert (1 oz.)	85
Cheddar (1 oz.)	115
cottage, creamed, 2%	
(¼ cup)	45
cottage, dry curd (¼ cup)	45
cream (1 oz.)	95
Neufchâtel (1 oz.)	70
Parmesan (1 tbsp.)	25
spread (1 oz.)	80
Swiss (1 oz.)	95
Cherries, canned (½ cup)	
sweetened	90
unsweetened	50
Cherries, fresh (½ cup)	70
Cherry, maraschino (1 large)	10
Chicken	
breast, fried (3 oz.)	170
liver, cooked (1 med.)	75
pot pie (4¼″ diam.)	535
roasted, no skin (3 oz.)	
dark meat	150
light meat	140
salad (3 heaping tbsp.)	185

Chili sauce (2 tbsp.)	35
Chocolate bar, plain (1 oz.)	150
Chocolate kisses (7)	150
Clams, canned (3 oz.)	85
Cocoa drink (8 oz.)	245
Coconut, shredded, (½ cup)	225
Cod, broiled (3 oz.)	145
Coleslaw (½ cup)	55
Cookies	
brownie with nuts (2″ sq.)	145
chocolate chip (1 med.)	50
oatmeal with raisins	
(3″ diam.)	65
sandwich-type (1 med.)	50
sugar (3″ diam.)	90
vanilla wafer (1 med.)	15
Cordials (1 cordial glass)	55-70
Corn, on the cob (5″ ear)	70
Corn, whole kernel (½ cup)	85
Corn bread (2″ sq.)	110
Crab (3 oz.)	85
Cranberry sauce, sweetened	
(½ cup)	200
Cucumber, raw (12 slices)	10
Cupcake, plain (2½″ diam.)	90
Custard (½ cup)	150
Dates (3 med.)	80
Deviled ham (1 tbsp.)	45
Doughnut (1 av.)	
cake-type or raised	125
cake-type, sugared	150
raised, jelly center	225
Duck, roasted, no skin	
(3 oz.)	265
Eclair, custard filled,	
chocolate icing (1 av.)	315
Egg (1)	80
Eggplant, raw (2 slices)	25
Fig, dried (1 large)	60
Fish sticks (3 oz.)	150
Frankfurter (2 oz.)	170
French toast (1 slice)	185
Fruit cocktail (½ cup)	
sweetened	75
unsweetened	40
Fudge (1″ sq.)	105
Gelatin, fruit flavored	
(½ cup)	70
Gingerbread (2″ sq.)	205
Graham cracker (2½″ sq.)	30
Grape juice, canned (½ cup)	80
Grapefruit (½ med.)	50
Grapefruit juice,	
unsweetened (½ cup)	50

Grapes (½ cup)	35	Noodles, cooked (½ cup)	100	Popover (1 av.)	110
Gumdrops (1 large or 8 small)	35	Nuts (¼ cup)		Popsicle (3 oz.)	70
		cashews, roasted	195	Pork, lean, trimmed	
Halibut, broiled (3 oz.)	145	peanuts, dry roasted	210	chop (3 oz.)	230
Hash, canned (½ cup)		peanuts, oil roasted	230	ham, cured (3 oz.)	160
corned beef	230	pecans	185	roast, loin (3 oz.)	215
roast beef	145	walnuts	200	sausage link (3 x ½″)	125
Honey (1 tbsp.)	65			spareribs, roasted	
Honeydew melon (¼ of 5″ diam.)	35	Oil, salad or cooking (1 tbsp.)	125	(about 6 med.)	245
		Old-fashioned (4 oz.)	180	tenderloin (3 oz.)	205
Ice cream, about 10% fat (½ cup)	130	Olives, green (4 med.)	15	Pork and beans in sweet sauce, canned (1 cup)	385
Ice cream soda (8 oz.)	260	Olives, ripe (3 small)	15	Pork and beans in tomato	
Ice milk, hardened (½ cup)	100	Onions (½ cup)	30	sauce, canned (1 cup)	310
Ice milk, soft-serve (½ cup)	135	Orange (1 med.)	75	Potato chips, 2″ diam. (10)	115
		Orange juice, unsweetened (½ cup)	60	Potatoes	
Jams and preserves (1 tbsp.)	55			au gratin (½ cup)	145
Jelly (1 tbsp.)	50	Pancake (4″ diam.)	60	cooked (2¼″ diam.)	80
Jelly beans (10)	65	Peach, fresh (1 med.)	35	frozen and heated (French fried), 2 x ½″ (10)	125
		Peaches, canned (½ cup)		hashed brown (½ cup)	230
Lamb, lean, trimmed (3 oz.)		sweetened	100	mashed, with milk (½ cup)	65
chop or roast, leg	160	unsweetened	40	scalloped (½ cup)	105
roast, shoulder	175	Peanut brittle (2½″ sq.)	110	sweet (½ cup)	120
Lemonade (½ cup)	55	Peanut butter (4 tbsp.)	380	Pretzels, stick, small (10)	10
Lettuce (2 large leaves)	10	Pear, fresh (1 med.)	100	Pretzels, thin, twisted (1)	25
Lima beans, dry, cooked (1 cup)	260	Pears, canned (½ cup)		Prune juice (½ cup)	100
Liquor, 80-90 proof (1½ oz.)	100-110	sweetened	100	Prunes (4 med.)	70
		unsweetened	40	Pudding (½ cup)	
Lobster (3 oz.)	80	Peas (½ cup)		chocolate	195
Lollipop (2¼″ diam.)	110	cow, blackeye, dry	95	tapioca cream	110
		green	60	vanilla or rice-raisin	140
Macaroni, cooked (½ cup)	95	split, dry	145		
Macaroni and cheese (1 cup)	430	Pepper, green, raw (1 med.)	15	Radishes (4 small)	5
		Pickle, dill (1 med.)	10	Raisins, dry (2 tbsp.)	60
Malted milk shake, chocolate (8 oz.)	500	Pickle, sweet (1 small)	20	Raspberries, fresh (½ cup)	35
Manhattan (3½ oz.)	165	Pie (1/7 of 9″ diam.)		Rhubarb, stewed, sweetened (⅓ cup)	190
Margarine, low calorie (refer to label)		apple, cherry, rhubarb	350	Rice, cooked (½ cup)	115
		blueberry	330	Roll (1 av.)	
Margarine, regular (1 tbsp.)	100	coconut custard	315	cloverleaf or pan	85
Marshmallow (1 large)	25	custard	285	frankfurter or hamburger	120
Martini (3½ oz.)	140	lemon meringue	305	hard	155
Meat loaf, beef and pork (4 x ⅜″ slice)	265	mince	365	sweet	180
		peach	360	Rye wafers, whole grain (2)	45
Milk (8 oz.)		pecan	490		
evaporated	345	pumpkin	275	Salad dressing (1 tbsp.)	
evaporated skim	190	Pineapple, canned (1 slice)		blue cheese or Roquefort	75
shake, chocolate	420	sweetened	90	French	65
skim	90	unsweetened	40	Italian	90
sweetened condensed	980	Pineapple, fresh (½ cup)	40	low-calorie (refer to label)	
2%	145	Pineapple juice, unsweetened (½ cup)	70	mayonnaise	100
whole	160	Pizza, cheese (5 oz.)	370	Thousand Island	80
Muffin (3″ diam.)	120	Pizza, sausage (7 oz.)	470	Salmon, broiled or baked (3 oz.)	155
Mushrooms, canned (¼ cup)	10	Plum, fresh (1 med.)	25	Salmon, canned pink (3 oz.)	120
Mustard, prepared (1 tsp.)	5	Popcorn, popped (1 cup)			
		plain	25		
		with oil and salt	40		

Saltine cracker (2″ sq.)	15	Soup, made with water (1 cup)		Tomato juice (½ cup)	25
Sandwich (2 slices bread, 1 tsp. butter)		split pea	145	Tomatoes, canned (½ cup)	25
bacon, lettuce, tomato	280	tomato	90	Tuna (3 oz.)	
egg salad	280	vegetable beef	80	canned in oil, drained	170
ham salad	320	Spaghetti, cooked (½ cup)	80	canned in water	110
tuna salad	280	Spaghetti, with meatballs and tomato sauce		Turkey, roasted, no skin (3 oz.)	165

Saltine cracker (2″ sq.) — 15
Sandwich (2 slices bread, 1 tsp. butter)
  bacon, lettuce, tomato — 280
  egg salad — 280
  ham salad — 320
  tuna salad — 280
Sauce (2 tbsp.)
  butterscotch — 205
  cheese — 65
  chocolate — 85
  gravy — 80
  tartar — 150
  tomato — 40
  white — 50
Sauerkraut (½ cup) — 20
Scallops, breaded and fried (3 oz.) — 165
Sherbet (½ cup) — 130
Shrimp (3 oz.)
  canned or cooked — 100
  French fried — 190
Soup, made with milk (1 cup)
  clam chowder — 210
  cream of chicken — 180
  cream of mushroom — 215
  cream of shrimp — 245
  oyster stew — 200
  tomato — 175

Soup, made with water (1 cup)
  split pea — 145
  tomato — 90
  vegetable beef — 80
Spaghetti, cooked (½ cup) — 80
Spaghetti, with meatballs and tomato sauce
  canned (1 cup) — 260
  home recipe (1 cup) — 330
Spinach, cooked (½ cup) — 20
Spinach, raw (1 oz.) — 10
Squash (½ cup)
  summer — 15
  winter — 65
Stew, beef and vegetable (1 cup) — 210
Strawberries (½ cup)
  fresh — 30
  frozen, sweetened — 140
Sugar
  brown (½ cup) — 410
  confectioners' (1 tbsp.) — 30
  granulated (1 tbsp.) — 40
Syrup (1 tbsp.)
  corn, light or dark — 60
  maple — 50
Tangerine (1 med.) — 40
Tomato, fresh (1 med.) — 40

Tomato juice (½ cup) — 25
Tomatoes, canned (½ cup) — 25
Tuna (3 oz.)
  canned in oil, drained — 170
  canned in water — 110
Turkey, roasted, no skin (3 oz.) — 165
Veal, lean, trimmed (3 oz.)
  chop — 175
  cutlet — 185
  roast — 145
Waffle (7″ diam.) — 210
Watermelon (4 x 8″ wedge) — 115
Wine (3 oz.)
  champagne (domestic) — 65
  muscatel, port, sherry — 130-140
  sauterne — 75
  vermouth, dry — 75-100
  vermouth, sweet — 120-135
Worcestershire sauce (2 tbsp.) — 25
Yogurt (½ cup)
  fruit — 120
  plain — 65
Zwieback (1 piece) — 30

INDEX